ECOTOURISM:
PRINCIPLES, PRACTICES & POLICIES
FOR SUSTAINABILITY

Megan Epler Wood

UNEP

United Nations Environment Programme
Division of Technology, Industry and Economics
Production and Consumption Unit
Tour Mirabeau, 39-43, quai André-Citroën
75739 Paris Cedex 15, France
Tel: 33 1 44 37 76 12. Fax: 33 1 44 37 14 74
e-mail: uneptie@unep.fr
www.uneptie.org/tourism/home.html

THE INTERNATIONAL
ECOTOURISM SOCIETY

The International Ecotourism Society
P.O. Box 668, Burlington, VT 05402 USA
Tel. 802/651-9818. Fax: 802/651-9819
e-mail: ecomail@ecotourism.org
www.ecotourism.org

UNITED NATIONS PUBLICATION

ISBN: 92-807-2064-3

Table of Contents

Foreword

"Putting tourism on a sustainable path is a major challenge, but one that also presents a significant opportunity".

KLAUS TÖPFER, UNEP Executive Director.

Ecotourism has been growing rapidly over the last decades. Yet, while ecotourism has the potential to create positive environmental and social impacts, it can unfortunately be as damaging as mass tourism if not done properly.

Typically located in pristine, fragile ecosystems, ecotourism projects run the risk of destroying the very environmental assets on which they depend. The loss of biodiversity and wildlife habitats, the production of waste and polluted effluent in areas that have little or no capacity to absorb them are just some of the worries. Furthermore, serious concerns about ecotourism exist as regards the degree of social fairness involved, and that of stakeholder involvement and control.

Recognizing the global importance of the issue, the United Nations designated 2002 as the International Year of Ecotourism, and the Commission on Sustainable Development (CSD) mandated the United Nations Environment Programme (UNEP) and the World Tourism Organization to carry out activities for the Year. Its goal is to review the lessons learned in implementing ecotourism, and to identify and promote forms of ecotourism that lead to the protection of critically endangered ecosystems, sharing the benefits of the activity with local communities and respecting local cultures.

The last three Conferences of the Parties to the UN Convention on Biological Diversity's have dealt with tourism's contribution to the sustainable use of biodiversity. They have also stressed that tourism generates significant revenues, and that as a growing percentage of the activities are nature-based, ecotourism does present a significant potential for realizing benefits in terms of the conservation of biodiversity and the sustainable use of its components.

As a contribution to the International Year of Ecotourism, UNEP and the International Ecotourism Society have jointly prepared this guide that should act as a basic resource book for governments and practitioners who want to develop environmentally and socially sound ecotourism practices. It includes background data and reference sources as well as practical guidelines. Case studies illustrate how these guidelines can be applied. The document has benefited from inputs by academia, and a broad range of experts coming from NGOs, inter-governmental agencies and ecotourism practitioners at both the international and local level. UNEP hopes it will provide useful insights to readers and we will welcome all comments or suggestions for another edition.

Putting ecotourism on a truly sustainable path is a major challenge, requiring partnership and cooperation between the tourism industry, governments, local people and the tourists themselves. With your help, we can achieve the ambitious goals set for the International Year of Ecotourism.

Mrs JACQUELINE ALOISI DE LARDEREL
Assistant Executive Director
Director, Division of Technology, Industry
and Economics (DTIE)
United Nations Environment Programme (UNEP)

We would like to acknowledge our technical reviewers, whose useful comments helped us generate a better publication. We are deeply indebted to Patricia Barnett (Tourism Concern), Sylvie Blangy, Ken Chamberlain, Claude Martin (WWF International), Michael Meyer (ETE), Laura Meszaros (UNEP/DEC), Nina Rao (Equations and the CSD-7 Southern Tourism Caucus), Wolfgang Strasdas, Niclas Svenningsen (UNEP/ROAP), Frank Vorhies (IUCN), Eugenio Yunis and Gabor Vereczi (WTO/OMT) and Hamdallah Zedan and Alexander Heyendael (CBD).

TIES acknowledgements
Jeremy Garrett: Editor
Lynnaire Sheridan: Case Studies and Resource Lists
Wolfgang Strasdas: Graphics
Also thanks to: Maggie Bowman, Elizabeth Halpenny, Nicole Otte, Patricia Carrington

Cover photos: Megan Epler Wood, Khary Bruning.
Text photo credits
Megan Epler Wood: *pages 7, 8, 12 (Philippines), 18, 21, 24, 27, 29, 31, 35, 40, 42, 43, 47, 56.*
Chandra Gurung: *pages 12 (Nepal), 23.*
Khary Bruning: *page 9.*

Tortilis Camp: *page 13.*
Kapawi: *page 19.*
International Expeditions: *page 17.*
Albert Teo: *page 38.*
Kingfisher Bay: *page 53.*

Introduction

Entering a national park by boat, Bolivia

Travel and tourism are among the world's fastest growing industries and are the major source of foreign exchange earnings for many developing countries. The World Tourism Organization (WTO) reports that receipts from international tourism grew by an average annual rate of 9% between 1988-1997. The number of international tourist arrivals reached more than 664 million in 1999 (well over 10% of the world's population), and international arrivals are expected to reach 1 billion by 2010. The increasing economic importance of tourism has captured the attention of most countries. However, the global growth of tourism poses a significant threat to cultural and biological diversity.

Ecotourism is a growing niche market within the larger travel industry, with the potential of being an important sustainable development tool. With billions of dollars in annual sales, ecotourism is a real industry that seeks to take advantage of market trends. At the same time, it frequently operates quite differently than other segments of the tourism industry, because ecotourism is defined by its sustainable development results: conserving natural areas, educating visitors about sustainability, and benefiting local people.

Market research shows that ecotourists are particularly interested in wilderness settings and pristine areas. According to the fifth meeting of the Conference of the Parties to the Convention on Biological Diversity, ecotourism has a unique role to play in educating travelers about the value of a healthy environment and biological diversity. However, proper planning and management are critical to ecotourism's development or it will threaten the biological diversity upon which it depends.

In the last 10 years, travel experiences in fragile natural and cultural areas have benefited from a variety of innovative small-scale, low-impact solutions offered by ecotourism – some of which will be documented in this package. These approaches have had an influence on the larger tourism market, but ecotourism will never transform the tourism industry, nor can it be a perfect model in every instance. Like all forms of sustainable tourism, it is a dynamic field, with new techniques and approaches evolving every year. A wide variety of stakeholders must be involved in its implementation – including business, government, non-governmental organizations and local communities. Responsible businesses must be encouraged to manage tourists properly with guidelines, certification and regulation. And local destinations must be ready to properly fund ecotourism management, or they will risk damaging their natural and cultural resources and, ultimately, their position in a rapidly growing international market.

Local communities have the most at stake, and therefore the most to lose, in the emerging international ecotourism marketplace. As globalization makes local economic control increasingly difficult, ecotourism seeks to reverse this trend by stressing that local business owners and local communities must be vitally involved. Opportunities to involve rural communities in tourism have attracted attention and raised many expectations, but the risks are great unless proper preparations are made. Local people must be informed in advance of all the possible consequences

Local ecotourism project, Belize

of tourism development, and they must formally consent to development in their areas.

The underlying concepts and principles behind ecotourism have helped set new standards for the tourism industry, and these standards continue to evolve. Many aspects still need to be fully addressed during implementation, and as answers to some of these questions arise from the field, the quick global dissemination of results is a priority. This document provides a short introduction to ecotourism, providing a look at the progress made in the last decade, and what will be needed to make it sustainable in the future.

This report is not intended to be academic in format or style. References used are catalogued in the list of resource documents at the end of the book along with a list of resource organizations.

Rain forest canopy walkway, Malaysia

What is Ecotourism?

Jaguar Preserve, Belize

Ecotourism has been defined as a form of nature-based tourism in the marketplace, but it has also been formulated and studied as a sustainable development tool by NGOs, development experts and academics since 1990. The term ecotourism, therefore, refers on one hand to a concept under a set of principles, and on the other hand to a specific market segment. The International Ecotourism Society (TIES) (previously known as The Ecotourism Society (TES)) in 1991 produced one of the earliest definitions:

"Ecotourism is responsible travel to natural areas that conserves the environment and sustains the well being of local people."

IUCN (now called the World Conservation Union) states in 1996 that ecotourism:

"is environmentally responsible travel and visitation to relatively undisturbed natural areas, in order to enjoy and appreciate nature (and any accompanying cultural features - both past and present) that promotes conservation, has low negative visitor impact, and provides for beneficially active socio-economic involvement of local populations."

Ecotourism as a Concept

Ecotourism is a sub-component of the field of sustainable tourism. *Figure 1* offers a reflection of where ecotourism can be placed within the process of developing more sustainable forms of tourism. This figure also provides a demonstration of how ecotourism is primarily a sustainable version of nature tourism, while including rural and cultural tourism elements.

Ecotourism aspires in all cases to achieve sustainable development results. However, it is important to clarify that all tourism activities – be they geared to holidays, business, conferences, congresses or fairs, health, adventure or ecotourism – should aim to be sustainable. This means that the planning and development of tourism infrastructure, its subsequent operation and also its marketing should focus on environmental, social, cultural and economic sustainability criteria.

Components of Ecotourism

- Contributes to conservation of biodiversity.
- Sustains the well being of local people.
- Includes an interpretation / learning experience.
- Involves responsible action on the part of tourists and the tourism industry.
- Is delivered primarily to small groups by small-scale businesses.
- Requires lowest possible consumption of non-renewable resources.
- Stresses local participation, ownership and business opportunities, particularly for rural people.

The strong orientation of the ecotourism field toward the evolution of principles, guidelines, and certification based on sustainability standards gives it an unusual position in the tourism field. Over the years, discussion in conferences has provided a general consensus on the components of ecotourism *(as seen in box above)*.

Ecotourism as a Market Segment

Ecotourism is a small but rapidly growing industry working within a niche market that is governed by market forces and regulations. Ecotourism is primarily advertised as being equivalent to nature tourism in the marketplace. Some countries, companies and destinations have social and environmental policies and programs, while others do not. This has led to confusion worldwide about the meaning of the term ecotourism as it is applied in the marketplace. Further discussion of guidelines and accreditation systems relating to sustainability criteria for the ecotourism industry can be found later in this chapter.

Figure 2 provides a reflection of how ecotourism fits into the larger tourism marketplace. Both adventure

Figure 1
ECOTOURISM AS A SUSTAINABLE DEVELOPMENT CONCEPT

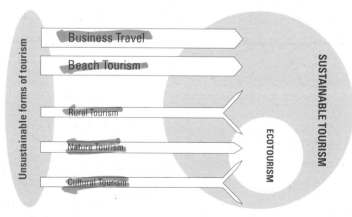

Strasdas 2001 (drawn by M. Meier)

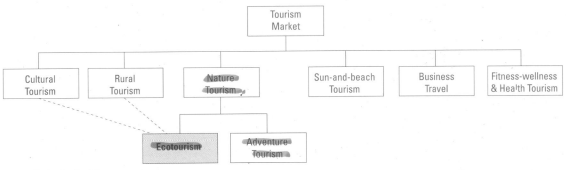

Figure 2
ECOTOURISM AS A MARKET SEGMENT

WTO, modified by Strasdas 2001

tourism and ecotourism are shown as subcomponents of nature tourism, while ecotourism has stronger links to rural and cultural tourism than adventure tourism.

In ecotourism the prime motivation is the observation and appreciation of natural features and related cultural assets, whereas in adventure tourism it is rather the physical exercise and challenging situations in natural environments.

From a functional viewpoint, ecotourism in the marketplace is mostly individual or small-scale tourism (tour groups up to 25, and hotels with less than 100 beds) that is operated by small- and medium-sized companies in natural areas. It represents a segment of the marketplace that concentrates on leading and accommodating small groups in natural areas in an educational manner using interpretive materials and local specialist guides.

The Roots of Ecotourism

With a history deeply rooted in the conservation movement, ecotourism has provided a highly strategic source of revenue to natural areas that need protection. Ecotourism began as an untested idea that many hoped could contribute to the conservation

of natural resources worldwide. Research undertaken in Kenya in the 1970s (*Thresher 1981*) demonstrated that the economic benefits of wildlife tourism far surpassed hunting – an activity that was banned in Kenya in 1977. In the early 1980s, rain forests and coral reefs became the subject of both innumerable studies by biologists interested in biological diversity and of a plethora of nature film documentaries. This interest helped launch a wide variety of local small businesses specializing in guiding scientists and filmmakers into remote zones. As these small businesses quickly began to prosper in countries such as Costa Rica and Ecuador, a more formal industry soon evolved to meet the needs of small tourism groups that were primarily composed of birdwatchers and committed naturalists. In many areas of the world, pioneer entrepreneurs created special field visits and studies for adult travelers, students and volunteers.

International nature-based businesses began to thrive in the 1980s with the growing interest in outdoor travel and the environment, spurred by excellent new outdoor equipment for camping and hiking, and events such as Earth Day. These companies began to realize that they could take the initiative to conserve the environment by sponsoring

Tourists enjoying tea house, Nepal

local conservation groups in the destinations they visited or by raising funds for local causes. They soon learned that training and hiring local people to run their businesses was the best way to manage their operations, and an excellent way of creating significant benefits for local people. Tour operators selling trips to the Galapagos Islands, Costa Rica, Kenya and Nepal were some of the early players in this movement. Some of these companies argue that, in fact, they had already been using ecotourism principles for some 20 to 30 years.

Because so many individuals with unique ideas and creative approaches are involved, it is rarely carried out the same way twice. Ecotourism is a business and can be profitable, but it should be a responsible business that aims to meet higher social and environmental goals. As such, ecotourism is highly dependent on the commitment of individual business owners who must be willing to apply a unique set of standards to their business approaches – standards that have only evolved in the last 10 years. The fact

that no international regulatory body exists, and that standards in the field of ecotourism are quite difficult to measure, has allowed businesses and governments to promote ecotourism without any oversight. Many travel and tourism businesses have found it convenient to use the term "ecotourism" in their literature, and governments have used the term extensively to promote their destinations, all without trying to implement any of the most basic principles explained in this document. This problem of "greenwashing" has undermined the legitimacy of the term ecotourism. Some greenwashing, though certainly not all, is the result of a lack of understanding of the underlying principles of ecotourism. International conferences, workshops and publications have made some advances in educating governments and businesses about ecotourism, but the misuse of the term remains a problem worldwide.

Many people often ask why ecotourism should be viewed differently from other forms of sustainable tourism. In essence, ecotourism must be planned and managed to successfully offer its key social and environmental objectives. This requires:

Birdwatchers in wetlands, Philippines

1. Specialized marketing to attract travelers who are primarily interested in visiting natural areas.
2. Management skills that are particular to handling visitors in protected natural areas.
3. Guiding and interpretation services, preferably managed by local inhabitants, that are focused on natural history and sustainable development issues.
4. Government policies that earmark fees from tourism to generate funds for both conservation of wild lands and sustainable development of local communities and indigenous people.
5. Focused attention on local peoples, who must be given the right of prior informed consent, full participation and, if they so decide, given the means and training to take advantage of this sustainable development option.

Tourist viewing Mt Kilimanjaro, Kenya

Principles of Ecotourism

Because ecotourism was originally just an idea, not a discipline, many businesses and governments promoted it without an understanding of its most basic principles. Establishing internationally and nationally accepted principles, guidelines and certification approaches proceeded throughout the 1990s but at a modest pace, because the process involves stakeholders from many regions, disciplines and backgrounds. Each region affected by ecotourism should develop its own principles, guidelines and certification procedures based on the materials already available internationally. This process of creating international certification guidelines is far from being completed.

The International Ecotourism Society has tracked the results of stakeholder meetings since 1991 to develop the set of principles on page 14, which are being embraced by a growing constituency of NGOs, private sector businesses, governments, academia and local communities.

Once principles have been agreed upon, specific guidelines can be developed that help define the market's best possible performance. Guidelines offer practical approaches to achieving sustainable development results, as gleaned from survey research on best practices and stakeholder meetings among researchers, the private sector, NGOs and local communities. International review finalizes the guidelines process, helping to assure that a wide variety of viewpoints are incorporated.

As ecotourism guidelines are being developed, it is important to consider some issues that may not be fully addressed by practitioners globally, such as:
1. The amount of control that traditional/indigenous communities retain when ecotourism is developed in natural areas that they manage or inhabit.
2. The efficiency and social fairness of current concepts of protected areas (which are central

13

Principles of Ecotourism

- Minimize the negative impacts on nature and culture that can damage a destination.
- Educate the traveler on the importance of conservation.
- Stress the importance of responsible business, which works cooperatively with local authorities and people to meet local needs and deliver conservation benefits.
- Direct revenues to the conservation and management of natural and protected areas.
- Emphasize the need for regional tourism zoning and for visitor management plans designed for either regions or natural areas that are slated to become eco-destinations.
- Emphasize use of environmental and social base-line studies, as well as long-term monitoring programs, to assess and minimize impacts.
- Strive to maximize economic benefit for the host country, local business and communities, particularly peoples living in and adjacent to natural and protected areas.
- Seek to ensure that tourism development does not exceed the social and environmental limits of acceptable change as determined by researchers in cooperation with local residents.
- Rely on infrastructure that has been developed in harmony with the environment, minimizing use of fossil fuels, conserving local plants and wildlife, and blending with the natural and cultural environment.

to ecotourism) for long-term conservation of biological and cultural diversity.

3. The risk that unregulated tourists contribute to lowering genetic capital and traditional knowledge belonging to traditional communities; i.e. biopiracy.

4. How to balance the needs of medium- and large-scale investors, often outsiders to local communities, with local expectations in participation with small-scale efforts for community-based tourism.

Ecotourism Guidelines for Nature Tour Operators was published in 1993 by The International Ecotourism Society, setting a standard for this sector of the industry. These guidelines have been distributed worldwide, and reprinted by dozens of organizations in numerous languages. Evaluation forms reveal that they have widespread acceptance from the industry, NGOs and academics. TIES will publish guidelines for ecolodges and marine ecotourism in 2002.

The Association for Ecological Tourism in Europe published recommendations in 1997 for environmentally oriented tour operators, and many local organizations, such as Alianza Verde in the Guatemalan region of the Peten, have developed ecotourism guidelines for all stakeholders with a local approach. Development of guidelines around the world has been a useful step to help local stakeholders address questions of how to develop ecotourism in local communities, ecosystems or in specific sectors of the industry, such as accommodations or tour operations. This can help to solve the problem of greenwashing, but ultimately, certification will be a fundamental tool to ensure businesses are meeting ecotourism standards.

Efforts to certify ecotourism are in their infancy. Certifying ecotourism industries involves gathering data from companies on their environmental and social performance, and then verifying these data. As ecotourism further defines itself through its stakeholders and in the marketplace, many questions remain about how well ecotourism can be certified, given that ecotourism businesses are small, highly dispersed and regional in character. Many are found in developing countries, where monitoring services and even communication systems may not be available. Ecotourism enterprises

Nature Tour Operator Guidelines

- **Prepare travelers.** One reason consumers choose an operator rather than travel independently is to receive guidance: How can negative impacts be minimized while visiting sensitive environments and cultures? How should one interact with local cultures? What is an appropriate response to begging? Is bartering encouraged?
- **Minimize visitor impacts.** Prevent degradation of the environment and/or the local culture by offering literature, briefings, leading by example and taking corrective actions. To minimize accumulated impacts, use adequate leadership and maintain small groups to ensure minimum group-impacts on destination. Avoid areas that are under-managed and over-visited.
- **Minimize nature tour company impacts.** Ensure managers, staff and contract employees know and participate in all aspects of company policy that prevent impacts on the environment and local cultures.
- **Provide training.** Give managers, staff and contract employees access to programs that will upgrade their ability to communicate with and manage clients in sensitive natural and cultural settings.
- **Contribute to conservation.** Fund conservation programs in the regions being visited.
- **Provide competitive local employment.** Employ locals in all aspects of business operations.
- **Offer site-sensitive accommodations.** Ensure that facilities are not destructive to the natural environment and particularly that they do not waste local resources. Design structures that offer ample opportunity for learning about the environment and that encourage sensitive interchanges with local communities.

The International Ecotourism Society, *Ecotourism Guidelines for Nature Tour Operators*, 1993

Proposed Guidelines for Successful Ecotourism Certification

- Indicators for sustainability must be arrived at by research of appropriate parameters based on current best practice.
- Indicators for sustainability must be reviewed and approved via a stakeholder process.
- Indicators for sustainability must be arrived at for each segment of the industry, e.g. hotels, tour operators, transportation systems, etc.
- Indicators for sustainability will vary according to region and must be arrived at via local stakeholder participation and research.
- Certification programs require independent verification procedures that are not directly associated with the entity being paid to certify. University involvement is ideal for this process.
- Certification programs, particularly for the small ecotourism business sector, are unlikely to pay for themselves through fees, and will need national, regional or international subsidization.
- Certification programs can be given to the operating entity, but should specify the products or locations that fulfill relevant criteria as certified.
- Certification should be ground tested before full-fledged implementation to ensure all systems are properly in line, due to the difficulty of verifying appropriate performance standards without advance testing.

Epler Wood and Halpenny, *Ecolabels in Tourism*, 2001

Ecotourism Certification – A Case Study from Australia

Australia's National Ecotourism Accreditation Program (NEAP) is an industry initiative of the Ecotourism Association of Australia, with funding from the Office of National Tourism. NEAP was revised and relaunched in March 2000 with a new sub-program for nature-based tourism. Its accreditation now has three levels: nature tourism, ecotourism and advanced ecotourism.

A performance-based accreditation program, NEAP requires that products of program participants achieve specific goals that are classified under specific categories: natural area focus, interpretation, ecological sustainability, contributions to conservation, work with local communities, cultural component, client satisfaction and responsible marketing. To attain the ecotourism accreditation level, the product must meet all core criteria in each category. Achieving advanced ecotourism status requires that the product meet 80% of bonus criteria.

The tourism operator or facility owner must complete an extensive form that addresses each criteria. In its first phase, NEAP was entirely dependent on the honesty of the applicant. But the new program launched in March 2000 will develop mechanisms for random auditing of products. The greatest limitation of the NEAP program, according to research, is the poor consumer recognition of the program and its labels; as of January 2000, Australia had accredited 237 NEAP products. This program only certifies products, not tour operators or facilities.

Adapted from Buckley, *Ecolabels in Tourism*, 2001

are operating on a small scale and are probably best evaluated using criteria designed for their style of enterprise.

Efforts to certify ecotourism businesses have been led by Australia, which established a research program in 1994 and launched a federally funded initiative in 1996 that is the only ecotourism-specific certification program in the world.

Regardless of whether global certification programs are developed for ecotourism or for more general sustainable tourism, international guidelines detailing how to develop and manage such certification programs are urgently needed. The proposed guidelines for ecotourism certification, seen on page 15, were developed for a publication on ecolabels by TIES staff and for circulation to leading researchers worldwide for further comment.

TIES Guidelines.

The Ecotourism Experience

Blue and gold macaw

Ecotourism is a travel experience, first and foremost, that helps travelers come to a better understanding of unique natural and cultural environments around the world. Hundreds of specialized tours and lodges now exist in natural areas that allow small groups to see unique environments and cultures with local guides. These guides are trained to interpret the cultural and environmental settings that visitors are coming to discover. They also focus on helping travelers develop better instincts on how to travel and how to properly contribute toward environmental conservation, cultural survival and other important sustainable development issues. Finally, small ecotourism groups are informed how to minimize their environmental and cultural impacts. The ecotourism experiences that have seen the most success evolved from the innovations of scientists, architects and local community leaders.

For example:
• Wildlife field researchers made many breakthroughs in studying wildlife species in the 1980s, working with unique species such as whales, turtles, mountain gorillas, orangutans, macaws and harpy eagles. A variety of specialized tours were developed to bring visitors for the first time to these field locations to see these species. Many of these trips were originally in very rustic field stations, and travelers paid a fee to support conservation and research initiatives. As the programs evolved, a great deal of effort was placed in designing the tours to prevent impacts on the wildlife and culture of the regions.
• Research breakthroughs in fields such as tropical ecology, ethnobotany, whale and primate ecology, and the archeology of ancient civilizations have motivated travelers to meet the scientists involved and to help with research. Workshops and other educational programs now allow tourists to take part in intensive field seminars with the scientists themselves – and at the same time help pay for the research.
• Innovative entrepreneurs and architects began to design specialized low-impact lodges that allowed travelers to stay in relative comfort while having magnificent wildlife-viewing opportunities at their doorstep. Ecolodges specializing in innovative approaches that minimally impacted the natural environment were built on every continent, many powered by alternative energy, designed in harmony

Mayan ruins, Mexico

with the local environment, and using local materials and indigenous designs.

• Local people became shareholders and owners of ecolodges or nature inns, or ran local community-based ecotours. Community-run ecotourism programs emerged around the world, offering travelers the opportunity to learn about different cultures, the social and cultural threats that local people face, and their understanding of local ecology. These programs can assist local communities with health care, education and with maintaining local traditions.

• In rural environments with rich natural resources, especially in Europe, ecotourism can be a sustainable alternative to dwindling agriculture revenues, offering visitors a natural and rural experience and partially reversing economic deterioration.

Environmental Awareness and Ecotourism

All this fresh interest in the environment and local cultures has created a dynamic economic engine that can spur healthy economic growth in under-developed areas, but also may result in unsustainable growth followed by rapid downturns, called "boom-bust" cycles. Past history has shown that the boom-bust syndrome – in locations such as Hawaii or coastal Spain – were very destructive to the environment and for the local economy. Such economic cycles should be avoided, and are the antithesis of building a healthy and sustainable economy that benefits local people in the long term. Statistics and research confirm that an increasing number of travelers will be reaching remote ecotourism destinations with greater ease, at less cost and faster than ever before, indicating that some ecotourism destinations may become vulnerable to the exact same boom-bust cycles that have plagued more accessible destinations in the past.

While a variety of lifestyle research studies show that travelers are concerned about environmental conservation and the welfare of local people, their travel choices do not appear to be based on these outlooks. The consumers' need to make responsible travel choices is increasingly pivotal to the success of ecotourism objectives, making it highly important that they understand precisely what a good ecotourism experience is. Consumer education campaigns, such as The International Ecotourism Society's *Your Travel Choice Can Make A Difference*, help travelers distinguish between enterprises and destinations that make no effort to conserve, limit growth or benefit local people, and those that do. Consumer education and guidelines for the selection of ecotourism experiences will strengthen the legitimate ecotourism marketplace and diminish the effectiveness of false claims of environmental and social responsibility (i.e. greenwashing).

The Number of Ecotourists

Because ecotourism is defined by its objectives to conserve nature and contribute to local people, it has been difficult to measure. As yet, no in-depth studies have attempted to determine how many nature tourists are actually motivated to make travel decisions based on ecotourism principles. Ecotourism is widely researched as nature tourism, leading to false assumptions on the size of the market. Research on nature tourism has shown that as much as 50% of the total travel market wants to visit a natural area during a trip, which might include a short day stop in a national park. While this is a very

Aerial of ecolodge, Ecuador

large market, it is quite different from the market that is actually motivated to travel in small groups, learn about wildlife and culture with a local guide, and help support local conservation and sustainable development.

An extremely rough estimate of the world's international ecotourism arrivals would be seven percent of the tourism market (*Lindberg 1997*), or approximately 45 million arrivals in 1998 and 70 million expected for 2010. To this, one must add the substantial number of domestic visitors to natural areas.

Key ecotourism destinations have reported dramatic increases in visits to protected and other natural areas. Ecotourists have always been strongly attracted to national parks and protected areas. While simply visiting a park or natural area is nature tourism – not ecotourism – visitor trends to parks give an indication of the growth of ecotourism as well. Surveys from the early 1990s began to register the dramatic growth in tourism to national parks

in important ecotourism markets – showing an important shift in tourism preferences from the traditional destinations of Europe to a broader range of nature destinations, primarily in developing countries. Foreign visitors to Costa Rica's parks skyrocketed from 65,000 in 1982 to 273,000 in 1991 – a 30% annual increase.

Other countries quickly began to note similar trends. Australia undertook a thorough survey of its nature-based tourists in 1995 (*Blamey & Hatch 1998*) and these results strongly confirmed that national parks and reserves have "high appeal" among international visitors to Australia. Of the 1.7 million foreign visitors to Australia in 1995, 50% visited at least one national park during their stay – a 10% increase over the previous year.

Many other nature-based destinations have documented high growth rates throughout the 1990s (*see the following table*).

In preparation for 2002, designated by the United

Visitation Rates to Nature-based Destinations

Country	1990	1999 Increase	Total % Increase	Average Annual
South Africa	1,029,000	6,026,000	486%	19.3%
Costa Rica	435,000	1,027,000	136%	9.0%
Indonesia	2,178,000	4,700,000	116%	8.0%
Belize*	88,000	157,000	78%	6.0%
Ecuador	362,000	509,000	41%	3.5%
Botswana*	543,000	740,000	36%	3.1%

* Visitation rates available only from 1990 to 1998.

World Tourism Organization, *Tourism Highlights 2000*, 2000

Birdwatchers with guide, Peru

Nations as the *International Year of Ecotourism*, the World Tourism Organization is conducting market surveys in some European countries, with results available in late 2001.

Ecotourist Demographics

At present, hundreds of independent nature tourism companies in the U.S. and Canada handle well over one billion dollars in annual sales. A number of research studies provide excellent information on the clientele of North American companies, providing demographics and information on nature tourist motivations. Based on data collected by HLA and ARA Consulting firms, it has been possible to construct a nature tourist market profile of North American travel consumers seen on page 22.

A portion of this market is undoubtedly ecotourism in design and implementation, but it is still unknown how much. In well-documented ecotourism destinations – including Costa Rica, Ecuador, Belize, South Africa, Kenya, Botswana and Nepal – hundreds of tour operators and lodges receive nature tourists from around the world, but no ecotourism market research is yet available in published literature on these destinations, though all these countries do provide data on their nature tourism market.

European statistics do not provide clear data on the nature tourism market, even though demand for environmentally friendly products is clearly demonstrated there. Research indicates that Europeans are more likely to seek out rural tourism in Europe rather than nature tourism, because most of the European natural environment is not a wilderness landscape (*Blangy & Vautier 2001*). Northern Europeans in particular have consistently shown interest in tourism with high standards of sustainability as part of the package they purchase, and nature tourism is strongly developing as an outbound market for these countries and for England.

Although Europe is a vital tourist market, little data is available on European interests or attitudes towards nature-based travel or ecotourism. Australian research (*Blamey 1998*) on its inbound nature-based market demonstrates that a high percentage of German (20%), Swiss (23%) and Scandinavian (18%) tourists were interested in Australia because of its nature-based outdoor activities. The European market interest in nature travel exceeded any other inbound market, including the U.S and Canada. This clearly indicates that Europe will be an important nature tourism outbound market, if European market research begins to identify nature and ecotourism as a category of research.

More research on the ecotourism market is necessary to better define what portion of the large and growing nature tourism market will most likely respond to social and environmental approaches and be willing to pay for them. Research shows that while consumers support environmental issues, they have been more enthusiastic about expressing their concern in surveys than about purchasing green products (*Ackerstein & Lemon 1999*). Future market research should distinguish between nature tourism and ecotourism, which requires a more sophisticated survey instrument that examines lifestyles and a consumer's willingness to pay for environmental and social sustainability approaches, not simply the activities the tourist has participated in. The question that remains is how many tourists in the 21st century will be willing to pay for environmentally and socially designed ecotourism programs. Such research will assist practitioners in designing programs for this market.

Explanation of an Ecotour

Today, many responsible ecotour operators are working successfully around the globe to create well-planned, interactive learning experiences that introduce small groups of travelers to new environments and cultures, while minimizing negative environmental impacts and supporting conservation efforts. These service providers can be local or international, and range from seasonal community-run and family operations to medium-scale outbound operators with yearly revenues in the millions of dollars.

However, most countries probably have more tour operators that do not follow responsible guidelines than those that do. Additionally, tour operators have been hesitant to develop their own reporting systems, making it difficult to statistically document ecotourism's overall performance. One progressive example of ecotourism certification standards, however, is Australia's National Ecotourism Assessment Program, with nearly 200 operator and lodge owner participants.

Case study evidence from the field shows that ecotour operators are seeking to provide small – to medium – sized donations to small NGOs operating in their destinations, and to assist with the development of new regional organizations that advocate sustainable tourism policies. Funds are primarily given for land conservation and community development.

Characteristics of A Good Ecotour

- Provides information prior to the trip on the culture and environments to be visited.
- Offers guidelines on appropriate dress and behavior in writing before departure and verbally during the tour.
- Offers in-depth briefing upon tourist's arrival of the destination's geographical, social and political characteristics, as well as its environmental, social and political challenges.
- Offers in-depth guiding throughout the trip with well-trained local guides.
- Offers the opportunity to meet and interact with local communities in a setting that is clearly not just a commercial venue for shopping or sales.
- Develops an understanding of both the local people's daily life and traditions, and the types of issues that are appropriate to discuss, well in advance of community interactions.
- Provides opportunity for contributions to local NGOs.
- Ensures that all park entry fees are paid in full.
- Offers site-sensitive accommodations.

A survey of The International Ecotourism Society's supporting members in 1998 revealed that small donations equalling US$1 million were given by leading tour operators to locally run NGOs in the 1990s, while at the same time many owner/operators helped establish regional associations that advocate for sustainable tourism policies, such as the Alaska Wildland Recreation and Tourism Association in Alaska, U.S., the Galapagos Tour Operator Association in Ecuador, and the Asociacion de Kayakismo y Ecoturismo in Baja, Mexico. Other owner operators supported indigenous organizations through specially designed NGOs, such as Fundacion Pachamama and Accion Amazonia in Ecuador, both founded in the mid-1990s. While others gave directly to land conservation initiatives and protected areas, such as two Costa Rica-based tour operators who donated $25,000 to the Costa Rica Park Service in the early 1990s to help with a funding crises, and a U.S.-based tour operator that helped establish the ACEER Foundation in the Peruvian Amazon which has conserved over 100,000 hectares of rain forest for biodiversity

research through private donations and tourism activities.

Ecotourism operators also directly support protected areas through gate fees. A 1994 international survey of protected areas showed that developing countries receive 54% of their revenue from tourism entrance fees (*Giongo 1993*). In Rwanda in the 1980s, tour operators paid $170 per client for small groups visiting mountain gorillas,

Overcrowding of tents, Nepal

resulting in more than $1 million in annual revenue to the Parc de Volcans. This was achieved while the park strictly limited the number of visitors and devoted funds to environmental education efforts across the country (*Lindberg 1991*).

Well-regulated protected areas, such as the Galapagos Islands of Ecuador, have directly benefited from entry fees paid by nature and ecotourism companies on behalf of their clients and also from license fees for boats. In 1998, nearly 65,000 travelers visited the Galapagos Islands, with Ecuadorian nationals paying $6 to enter and foreigners paying $80. Visitor entrance fees totaled $4.3 million in that year, averaging $66 per visitor.

Largely because of the Galapagos Islands' entry fees, Ecuador's national park service has been able to manage this world heritage ecosystem while limiting visitation to reasonable numbers, requiring high-quality guiding services by local people, maintaining control of which islands and trails are visited by travelers, and providing some support to park management throughout the country. At the same time, Ecuadorians are able to visit and learn about their valuable natural heritage at a very equitable price, which has undoubtedly influenced many young people in the country to become involved in conservation.

Ecotours offer highly educational visits to the great natural destinations on the planet. Tour operators have been proactive in many instances by using their clout, time and revenue to support destinations. Fee systems are one of the most important ways that ecotourism operators can ensure that protected areas visited by their clients are properly valued by governments. It is highly important, however, that fees gathered by governments are directed toward the conservation and management of the protected areas that ecotourists are visiting.

Site for ecolodge, Egypt

Explanation of an Eco-destination

Ecotourists typically look for experiences that provide a sense of closeness to the natural attractions and local communities that first brought them to a destination. Any destination that seeks to attract these tourists must protect its resources while facilitating a sense of integration with the local community. It is commonly but incorrectly thought that the private sector is exclusively responsible for protecting the environment and local communities. But in fact, intervention of other stakeholders at the regional and national level is required. First and foremost, governments are responsible for planning, policy-making and zoning, which helps ensure that destinations are not overbuilt. Governments also are responsible for waste and water treatment systems and energy resources. As such, it is in their best interest to require more sustainable and environmentally sound approaches. If no effective regulation or enforcement of environmental laws exists, and if natural areas are developed without foresight, facilities will be improperly constructed in certain instances. Even in remote areas, where ecotourism is often developed, it is still necessary to set development standards that are approved in coordination with local stakeholders, particularly representatives of local communities.

If mega-tourism complexes are planned with built-up, walled-in complexes, golf courses, "guests-only" clubs, and "plantation-style" service, these same areas cannot be expected to be appropriate for ecotourism. The concept of an eco-destination is new, and no guidelines have been written for it. It emerged precisely because governments sought to promote ecotourism in destinations that already had been developed without any of the basic principles that might attract an ecotourist, and at times without respect for the environment or local communities. The worst examples of this type of destination development have been reported from Southeast Asia, where in one case, millions of ethnic peoples were resettled from their homelands and compensated with so-called "ecotourism" jobs in new locations. This was clearly not true ecotourism and shows how ecotourism can be mislabeled and mishandled by governments.

The planning and management of a destination will determine how well ecotourism can thrive

---

Entrance Fee Contribution to Protected Areas – A Case Study from Zimbabwe, India and Indonesia

A study undertaken by the International Institute for Environment and Development examined the current and potential tourism contributions to three national parks: Gonarezhou of Zimbabwe, Keoladeo of India, and Komodo of Indonesia.

While in each of these cases tourism was the greatest source of revenue, the actual financial contribution of entrance fees to park finances was minimal and in two of the parks the net contribution was negative. Government funding was actually subsidizing tourism. Because entrance fees provided a substantial proportion of tourism revenues, the study endorsed raising the fees to ensure that the cost of tourism was covered and that it would also contribute funds to conservation. The survey in Keoladeo National Park outlined that tourists would in fact pay more and the authors suggested raising park fees as the best management option.

Tourism can contribute to conservation in protected areas, but it needs to be effectively managed. This study shows that the economic impacts can also be evaluated to determine opportunities for greater benefit.

Goodwin *et al*, 1997

Eco-destination Characteristics

- Natural features conserved within a protected landscape.
- Low density development, where natural areas are abundant and the built landscape does not dominate.
- Evidence that tourism is not harming natural systems such as waterways, coastal areas, wetlands and wildlife areas.
- Thriving small community businesses, including food stands and other types of craft enterprises owned by local people.
- Plenty of designated outdoor recreation zones that are designed to protect fragile resources, including bike paths, trails or boardwalks that are shared by locals and visitors alike.
- Thriving, locally owned lodges, hotels, restaurants and businesses that provide genuine hospitality with friendly, motivated staff.
- A variety of local festivals and events that demonstrate an on-going sense of pride in the local community's natural environment and cultural heritage.
- Clean and basic public facilities for tourists and locals to share, such as public showers and toilets.
- Friendly interaction between local people and visitors in natural meeting places, such as local shops or benches by the sea.

there. However, it is still extremely rare to see integrated regional tourism planning and management, not to mention strategies that highlight ecological and social considerations. The planning of an eco-destination depends on baseline data of social and environmental factors, zoning strategies, regulations that can prevent deliberate abuse of fragile ecosystems, local participation in developing a set of standards for limits of acceptable change, and long-term monitoring.

Once clear planning for development takes place, it is much more plausible that individual businesses can succeed at their goals of offering environmentally sensitive tours and lodging that provide benefits to local communities. Management is absolutely required at the destination to ensure the long-term harmony of tours and lodges with the people and environment of the region.

Eco-destination Planning Guidelines

- Master plans for the entire tourism development region should specify green zones, trails, walking paths, public access areas, and clear rules on the density of development allowed in residential and commercial zones.
- Zones for tourism use should be clearly designated, as are zones inappropriate for tourism use.
- Visitor management plans and procedures should incorporate public comment during design and implementation phases, with monitoring programs that allow for regular discussion of tourism use and the correction of problems when they occur.
- Full stakeholder consultation should take place on the type of tourism development (if any) desired by local communities, utilizing local neutral intermediaries who understand the community's viewpoints and will not advocate a particular development approach. This process must give the community adequate time to consider its options, with outside counsel and representation available on request.
- Integrated natural resource planning should offer residents a variety of sustainable economic development alternatives beyond ecotourism.

Explanation of an Ecolodge

The term "ecolodge" was formally launched in the marketplace at the First International Ecolodge Forum and Field Seminar held in 1994 at Maho Bay Camps in the U.S. Virgin Islands. Formal dialogue at this conference resulted in *The Ecolodge Sourcebook for Planners and Developers* (*Hawkins* et al *1995*). The first *International Ecolodge Guidelines* (*Mehta* et al, *in press*) are the result of a 1995 international conference in Costa Rica and five years of research and international review.

This is the first book to offer a definitive international definition of an ecolodge.

It must be stressed that an ecolodge's value is as much in its setting as its structures. Ecolodges need a well-protected setting that is not plagued by over-development or resource destruction issues. The value of an ecotourism property rises and falls with its ability to protect substantial biodiversity, wildlife and pristine landscapes. Many ecolodges have established their own private reserves, enabling them to directly manage the natural resources they depend on for their business.

Ecolodges can be extremely rustic or very luxurious. Accommodations in general for the ecotourism industry are usually mid-range

Ecotourism planning workshop, Samoa

Ecolodge Definition

An ecolodge is a tourism accommodation facility that meets the following criteria:
- It conserves the surrounding environment, both natural and cultural.
- It has minimal impact on the natural surroundings during construction.
- It fits into its specific physical and cultural contexts through careful attention to form, landscaping and color, as well as the use of localized architecture.
- It uses alternative, sustainable means of water acquisition and reduces water consumption.
- It provides careful handling and disposal of solid waste and sewage.
- It meets its energy needs through passive design and combines these with their modern counterparts for greater sustainability.
- It endeavors to work together with the local community.
- It offers interpretative programs to educate both its employees and tourists about the surrounding natural and cultural environments.
- It contributes to sustainable local development through research programs.

Adapted from Mehta et al, *International Ecolodge Guidelines*, In Press

in price, though the range of accommodation types is enormous – from luxury tent-camps in Africa, to backpacker tents in Alaska, to rustic lean-tos and homestays in Belize, to ranches and haciendas in Venezuela, to tea houses in Nepal. Live-aboard boats also are popular, particularly on the Amazon.

High-end small cruise ships that can travel to idyllic marine environments such as Baja, Mexico, or Australia's Great Barrier Reef have also been extremely successful.

Many lodges offer their own guides and interpretation walks, as their visitors are frequently independent travelers that are not traveling with a tour guide. Often local farmers or indigenous people with in-depth knowledge of the local flora and fauna are hired to guide for ecolodges. Local guides usually are highly motivated by the unexpected opportunity to interpret the natural features of their home to outsiders, after years of surviving by poaching wildlife or laboring in unsustainable logging, agriculture or oil exploration. The local guide's knowledge of the land goes well beyond what most urban citizens have ever experienced in their lives, and this gives visitors a genuine respect for the people and places they are visiting. The interaction between host

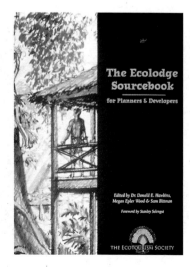

The Ecolodge
Sourcebook
for Planners & Developers

Edited by Dr. Donald E. Hawkins,
Megan Epler Wood & Sam Bittman
Foreword by Stanley Selengut

THE ECOTOURISM SOCIETY

Ecolodge Sourcebook

Visitors at ecolodge, Malaysia

and guest can lead to a whole new outlook for local people on the special nature of where they live.

Other recreation opportunities offered by lodges vary tremendously depending on the site: game drives, bird watching, canoeing, horseback riding, bicycling, beach trips and educational visits to locally run museums, zoos, butterfly farms, agricultural and livestock farms, craft production areas and other natural history and cultural sights. Some high-end lodges are creating jungle canopy walkways on their own properties as another guest amenity; these walkways provide unparalleled opportunities to explore the life above the rain forest tree-tops and in the most diverse part of the rain forest. Coordination of a fulfilling ecotourism itinerary requires an active working relationship with the local community. Ecolodges need to work with local guides and interact with the owners of different tourism resources – whether these are farms, canoes or horses – that would provide interesting day and half-day tours for visitors.

The management and operation of an ecolodge differs from a mainstream hotel for many reasons.

According to *International Ecolodge Guidelines* (*Mehta* et al, *in press*), the ecolodge is most often found in wilderness areas that are the least-developed, most-remote areas in any country; therefore, they are the last places to receive government investments in health, education, electricity, potable water, roads, etc. This poses a special challenge to the ecolodge owner or manager who must achieve sustainable development by supporting local communities in a long-term development program and putting a land-conservation program in place with a minimum of outside assistance. Education is one of the main mediums that will create successful ecotourism, and it falls to the ecotourism owner or manager to provide it.

Local Vendors

Local vendors in the ecotourism industry include food stands, restaurants, guiding services, vehicle rentals, taxis, recreation services (horses, boats and rafts, bikes, etc.) and craft producers/vendors. These types of service are most often offered by local community members. These vendors play a crucial role in the success of the ecotourism

Local field guide, Ecuador

Ecolodge Management Characteristics

- Provides on-the-job training to community members and local guides.
- Uses a majority of local staff people, and avoids giving city-trained or expatriate individuals all of the key responsibilities.
- Sets up after-hours second-language programs (to assist staff in speaking the language of visiting guests) using a local college graduate with expertise in language training.
- Has guests contribute to staff education and community development projects involving education or health.
- Encourages interested community members to communicate their knowledge about the area, while encouraging local guides to mingle with guests during communal hours.
- Supports guest learning experiences through visits to local farms, nurseries, reforestation projects, butterfly farms and other efforts to promote sustainability in the region.
- Promotes a system for guests to contribute financially to the preservation of natural areas in the region.
- Insists on recycling everything from table scraps to plastics, paper and metal.
- Uses alternative energy wherever possible.
- Uses biodegradable detergents and avoids the use of toxics whenever possible.
- Does not keep caged or exotic animals on the premises.

Adapted from Lewis, *International Ecolodge Guidelines*, In Press

product and its ability to benefit local communities. Many times, these businesses are very small and the owners need encouragement and a small amount of capital to get started. They can turn to NGOs or to the ecotourism industry itself to provide assistance with start-up businesses.

Ecotourism's economic contribution to local people must largely be evaluated based on the success of local vendors. These estimates vary greatly depending on the destination. Research from Belize (*Lindberg & Enriquez 1994*) indicates that more than 40% of local community members see economic benefits from nearby Hol Chan Marine Reserve, while Costa Rica studies (*Baez & Fernandez 1992*) estimate that less than 10% of local households benefit from visitors to Tortuguero National Park. The first location, the village of San Pedro in Belize, is well-known for a wide variety of small local businesses, from hotels to bars to clothing shops – all frequented by divers who have cash to spend. The second, Tortuguero, is characterized by all-inclusive lodges where visitors pay in advance, travel by boat in remote wetlands to view wildlife, and then simply return to lodges that are not owned by local people.

The problem of economic leakage is difficult to evaluate uniformly. In the case of Tortuguero, no small-scale economy of any kind exists – locals primarily survive on subsistence fishing, or they may have worked for nearby banana plantations in the past. A low diversity of goods in local communities, long dominated by large-scale plantations or cattle ranches, hurts their ability to benefit from ecotourism. In contrast, if tourist destinations contain more micro-enterprises, it is more likely that a larger percentage of local people will benefit.

In areas not characterized by small business, leakage can be reduced by lease fees, land rental fees, and other per person usage charges that return to local residents. In Kenya, the Maasai have long chosen to continue their pastoral lifestyle despite growing visitor numbers on or near their lands. They are not interested in small business, and their culture would actually be damaged if they were to become local vendors. In this case, the Maasai have begun

Fruit vendor, Tobago

to charge safari companies leases for the use of their land, a specialized concession fee that goes toward community needs. This enables them to continue with their traditional lifestyle while receiving direct income from ecotourism companies for the use of their land. This model has been successful, with Maasai group ranch managers even publishing annual reports for the community based on the revenues received from the fees.

Efforts to improve community entrepreneurship must therefore be based on local cultural needs. Local products must also be marketed with value-added approaches, using attractive packaging to call attention to the fact they are locally made or grown. Organic products have received particularly good reception in the ecotourism marketplace in such countries as Costa Rica and Belize. While local vending certainly provides an important opportunity to generate additional revenues, it is important that local products are

not undervalued. For example, communities in Amazonian Peru's Puerto Maldonado have many shops and local businesses, but only 26% of the community receives income, largely because of the modest nature of the vendors' products, and the fact that the backpacker market that frequents the area puts a low value on

Quinoa bar vendor, Peru

the community's simple services. However, a nearby lodge in Infierno that was developed for the mid-priced market has made the community a full partner in its enterprise, sharing 60% of the profits (*Stronza 2000*). The lodge is working with the community to develop a whole range of crafts to sell at the lodge at higher prices. Clearly this option provides Infierno's community with a much improved rate of return on their efforts and a much better outlook for their future.

The Components
of Successful Ecotourism

Ecotourism Stakeholders

The ecotourism sector of the travel industry is primarily a collection of small- and medium-sized local businesses, communities and non-governmental organizations that develop and implement ecotourism programs in remote and fragile destinations for both the group tour and independent traveler markets. They are serviced in part by outbound tour operators located primarily in developed countries that specialize in ecotourism. These operators provide the niche marketing and booking services for a significant proportion of organized ecotours worldwide.

For ecotourism to be properly implemented, local and international ecotourism stakeholders are dependent on government (particularly Ministries of Tourism and Environment) to develop policies that will protect and manage natural areas. Government tourism boards and ministries are also crucial players in establishing the reputation and "brand recognition" of the country as an ecotourism destination.

Ecotourism stakeholders also depend on the broader tourism industry to transport ecotourists and accommodate them upon arrival in the destination country, or for a part of their stay. After all, many tourists may only spend a portion of their time on an ecotour or in an ecolodge. Other important stakeholders include local authorities, who often regulate land-use and control key infrastructure, and protected area managers who are responsible for the management of visitors in fragile natural areas.

International development agencies also have an important role to play in ecotourism development because they finance projects relating to tourism development, the conservation of biological diversity, and micro-enterprise development – all issues closely related to ecotourism.

Finally, successful implementation of ecotourism depends on the development of a stable infrastructure. This includes currency exchange rates, transport systems, peace and security, and good telecommunications systems. A variety of government ministries are involved with providing a stable environment for business development, and their cooperation is no less important for ecotourism than for other types of international trade. Even though ecotourism businesses are located in remote natural areas, they still require much of the same infrastructure as other businesses to deliver quality experiences for their clients.

The stakeholder's role in developing successful ecotourism is reviewed here.

Ecotourism Industry

Travel Agents

Travel agents are located throughout the world and play an important role in marketing retail travel industry products but, perhaps surprisingly, have not played a significant role in marketing or sales for the ecotourism industry. In the past, outbound tour operators (*see below*) handled nearly all marketing and retail duties in the ecotourism industry. Now, the Internet is increasingly important as a sales medium for ecotourism products and is likely to further supplant the need for travel agents in this market niche. Recent reports by the Travel Industry Association of America show that travel planning is surging on the Internet. In 1999, more than 52 million online travelers used the Internet for this purpose – an increase of 54% over the previous year.

Outbound Tour Operators

Outbound tour operators are by far the ecotourism industry's dominant marketing and sales organizations. They create the brand name that sells the ecotourism products. They market destinations using four-color brochures, catalogues with photos of wildlife and ecosystems, World Wide Web pages and, in some cases, through the distribution of film, videotapes and CD-ROM disks. The outbound operator takes responsibility for selecting and packaging the tour product. They must oversee the creation of itineraries to ensure that they will meet the market demand. Outbound operators handle all sales of the tour product and also handle most air arrangements for their clients through in-house travel agents. They provide tourists with all essential pre-departure information and also are responsible for traveler insurance and liability issues.

Tour Operator Responsibilities

- Build environmental and cultural awareness through information and education for clients.
- Minimize impact on the environment.
- Provide direct financial benefits for conservation.
- Respect local cultures.
- Support local businesses and service providers.
- Provide local guide services and assist with training local guides.
- Manage activities in a responsible manner, using local guidelines for visitor behavior.
- Support parks and protected areas, paying entry fees at all times.
- Work in cooperation with local NGOs and government to develop plans for visitor management that protects local people and the environment.
- Avoid over-crowded, over-exploited destinations on itineraries and help develop lesser-known sites.
- Offer site-sensitive accommodations.

The International Ecotourism Society,
Ecotourism Guidelines for Nature Tour Operators, 1993

A common misunderstanding is that outbound tour operators handle all tour details throughout a trip – this is rare. Outbound operators usually contract inbound tour operators to deal with the specifics of a travel program once the client enters the destination country. The inbound operator (*see below*) usually represents the outbound operator, making it appear that the "brand-name" company is handling the tours throughout the client's travel experience.

Outbound tour operators, however, must also take responsibility for meeting ecotourism objectives as part of their responsibility to oversee their product. This may require extensive work with their inbound operators to ensure that guiding, business, conservation practices and host community relations concur with ecotourism guidelines.

It is important to note that while most outbound operators are private businesses, a substantial number are non-profit organizations providing ecotravel as a service for their members. While most non-profit travel programs in the U.S. market tours to their members, they still contract an outbound tour operator to provide the tour service. A survey of U.S.-based outbound tour operators in the early 1990s (*Higgins 1996*) indicated that 17% of their pre-packaged itineraries were arranged in cooperation with non-profit organizations. This trend has continued to advance rapidly throughout the 1990s according to many industry sources. A growing number of non-profit organizations are successfully marketing tours to their members, and tour operators are observing that their non-profit clients are extremely successful at marketing trips.

Inbound Tour Operators

Inbound tour operators usually are located in the major cities of destination countries, such as San Jose, Costa Rica; Quito, Ecuador; Kathmandu, Nepal; or Nairobi, Kenya. They handle multi-day group tours for outbound operators, but they also may offer alternative excursions for walk-in business. Their activities can even extend to providing conference services or customized itineraries directly to individual clients. Inbound operators may also, in some cases, own their own lodges or hotels, which they use for their tour clients.

Ecolodge Cabin, Kenya

The inbound operator takes the primary responsibility for the client during the trip. As such, they are the primary entity that is responsible for ensuring that any trip is of a high quality and, particularly, that the educational component meets ecotourism industry standards. To achieve this, inbound companies must have quality interpretive guides.

This is the key human resource that establishes an inbound operator as a top competitor in the marketplace, and it is particularly important to their outbound clients.

Ecotourism inbound operators need special support services, such as a network of comfortable but rustic

Ecolodge Owner/Manager Responsibilities

- Design the lodge to reflect the local natural and cultural environment, using the principles of sustainable design and endemic design styles.
- Use site planning to minimize the environmental impact of construction and to protect key natural features such as vegetation. Avoid use of non-renewable construction materials and use recycled building products whenever possible.
- Design an operational ecolodge that will minimize use of natural and, particularly, non-renewable resources. This could include energy and water reduction strategies but also a waste management plan that encourages reduction of excess waste through reuse and recycling.
- Work in collaboration with the local community and involve them in the planning of the ecolodge. Support the local economy and initiatives by contracting local service providers and buying local products. Offer local people employment that spans a wide range of responsibilities and incorporates them into management roles.
- Provide benefits to local conservation and research programs, either public or private.
- Work with government and local NGOs to develop long-term sustainable land-use plans.
- Offer visitors interpretive programs that will educate them about the local natural and cultural environment.
- Give clients the opportunity to contribute directly to local development and environmental projects.
- Investigate the economic and legal aspects of developing the ecolodge and run it as a business. A facility that operates in contravention of the law or is not financially viable will not effectively contribute to the conservation of the natural environment or benefit the local community.

Adapted from Mehta et al, *International Ecolodge Guidelines*, In Press

---

local cuisine and are owned by local entrepreneurs. They must also work with local vendors to ensure that tourists have an opportunity to view and ideally purchase genuine local products, such as handicrafts.

It is the inbound operator's responsibility to ensure that tourism products generate dollars for local conservation projects. They must work with local communities at each destination site visited to ensure that host communities have proper opportunities to benefit from the tourism program and that appropriate guest-host interactions exist.

Ecolodges

All ecolodges reflect the creative initiative and entrepreneurialism of business pioneers, rather than large multinational corporations. Found in nature tourism destinations around the world, each ecolodge tends to be individually owned rather than part of a chain. Some lodge owners depend on business from inbound tour operators to provide a steady, predictable client base, while others have established their own market base through direct marketing and public relations strategies.

In some cases, skilled entrepreneurs have partnered with indigenous landowners to co-manage the wild land resources that tourists visit and local people depend upon, thereby achieving a positive situation for both the lodge and the local people. Ecolodges also frequently contribute towards maintaining official protected areas, because they are often quite dependent on proper management of government-controlled reserves. Lodge owners may be involved in long-term agreements with protected areas worldwide, either as concessionaires that pay percentage fees

lodges that offer good backcountry experiences and excellent wildlife viewing, while meeting standards of environmental sustainability. They must select ground transportation services that are suitable in size for their small groups, and minimize energy usage and select restaurants that feature

Capacity Building in Brazil – A Case Study of Conservation International (CI)

Conservation International (CI) has made ecotourism one of several sustainable development alternatives to assist highly diverse regions. CI targeted Brazil, a nation of high biological diversity, as one of many important nations to develop capacity for delivering quality ecotourism. CI in 1994 initiated the Ecotourism Capacity Building Workshop program, which would conduct courses in regions with the greatest need for biodiversity conservation and areas with endangered ecosystems. Capacity building included three components: *Product Development* to train professionals with little theoretical knowledge of ecotourism; *Train the Trainer* to complement the first workshop and develop skills to conduct similar courses on ecotourism; and the *Leveling* and *Upgrading* workshops to provide advanced training and qualify participants as Regional Ecotourism Experts.

In the *Product Development* workshops, small groups of five to seven participants (determined by their knowledge of a target region, education, etc.) would develop an ecotourism business – either a tour operation or an ecolodge. To close the workshop, attendees participated in an ecotourism experience that solidified their understanding of all the course's concepts. The *Train the Trainers* program was crucial to the success of CI's ecotourism training. Tourism and environmental institutions selected participants with high credibility in their communities, who were good communicators and, administratively, who were able to facilitate an ecotourism course. The first course involved 35 people who now promote and facilitate ecotourism product development in their own regions.

When CI evaluated their program in 1996, the 600 survey responses indicated that 75% of workshop attendees applied the concepts they learned in their daily professional activities, 67% used the techniques taught to develop new ecotourism products (38% were new tour itineraries and 26% were new ecolodges), and 54% of participants have since created new ecotourism learning events in their regions.

Adapted from Hillel and de Oliveira, *Ecotourism Capacity Building Workshop*, 2000

to parks, as "friends" who are financial supporters of park initiatives, or as informal supporters that provide assistance on a project-by-project basis. These ecolodges may actively contribute to trail maintenance, volunteer research programs, clean-up days, or the monitoring of visitor use, depending on the local situation.

Non-Governmental Organizations

Non-governmental organizations (NGOs) play a prominent role in ecotourism development. They usually are involved for one of two reasons: 1) protection of biodiversity and environment, or 2) sustainable development for local people. NGOs are ideal partners for the private sector by developing a myriad of programs such as research on best practices, guide training, regional planning and stakeholder meetings, community development, protected area management, and targeted conservation initiatives.

NGOs also are actively working nationally and internationally to ensure that ecotourism is developing in a manner that is consistent with national and international conservation and sustainable development priorities. In fact, NGOs worldwide are increasingly developing their own ecotourism programs because of their strong desire to use ecotourism as a tool for conservation and sustainable development. For example, The Nature Conservancy, the largest private conservation organization in the world, has developed an ecotourism program that is assisting with the responsible development of ecotourism products, the planning of ecotourism for protected areas, and the development of user fees to assist with conservation and sustainable development with projects in Ecuador, Belize, Costa Rica, Guatemala, Jamaica, the Dominican Republic, Bolivia and Peru.

Finally, many local NGOs are implementing true grassroots ecotourism initiatives focused on the conservation of local resources that can benefit from ecotourism's economic and educational potential. Turtle-, whale-, penguin- and bird-watching programs, for example, are an excellent example of how ecotourism can successfully raise awareness and funds for protection, involve local guides and rangers, and lead to long-term sustainable conservation of an endangered species.

Communities

Communities have a vital stake in appropriate ecotourism development in their region, and their participation and involvement are critical to the process. The socioeconomic and cultural impacts of tourism are great, with several well-known negative impacts:

1. loss of local traditions;
2. commercialization of local cultural products;
3. erosion of self-worth;
4. undermining of family structure;
5. loss of interest (particularly among youth) in land stewardship;
6. fighting among those that benefit from the tourism cash economy and those that do not;
7. crime and adoption of illegal underground economies to serve tourists through prostitution, gambling and drugs.

Most researchers agree that some of these social ills can be prevented if the community gives its prior informed consent to any ecotourism projects in its area, participates in tourism development, and remains part of the planning process for tourism entering into the community. If ecotourism is to succeed as a viable form of sustainable development, the private sector, governments and NGOs all must cooperate to include local communities in the development process. Basic guidelines for community participation offer the approaches required to involve local communities.

The need to understand and evaluate a community in advance of proceeding with any partnership or development initiative is paramount, with many assessment approaches available for this purpose (*Ashley & Roe 1998, Lash* et al *in press*). Pre-assessment is important to ensure that community leaders objectively evaluate their needs and goals, and that they are not mistakenly swayed by the offer of funding or business opportunities that might later prove detrimental to the community.

Understanding the decision-making process of a community is highly important. Many local communities do not have a top-down decision-

Community-based boat builder, Malaysia

Basic Steps to Encourage Community Participation

- **Understand the Community's Role.** Communities should exercise control over their growth and development. They will in many cases need technical assistance to make appropriate decisions and should be given adequate information and training in advance. Allocate time, funds and experienced personnel to work with communities well in advance. Avoid allowing communities to feel they are powerless to influence patterns of development.

- **Empower Communities**. Participation is a process that is more than just making communities the beneficiaries of an ecotourism project. Jobs are an important benefit, but they do not replace empowerment. Communities must genuinely participate in the decision-making process. This involves more than just consultation. Processes must be initiated to ensure that communities can manage their own growth and resources wisely.

- **Urge Local Project Participation.** Project managers must identify local leaders, local organizations, key priorities of the community, and ideas, expectations and concerns local people already have. Information can be gathered for and by the community. The opinions gathered should be disseminated and discussed with the community along with other relevant information such as government market statistics or regional development plans. Training opportunities must be formulated at this phase to help community members gain planning skills, and also the entrepreneurial skills required to run small businesses.

- **Create Stakeholders.** Participation can be encouraged at two levels – for individuals and for local organizations. Investment in project development areas should be encouraged, either in cash, labor or in-kind resources. Developing lodging by local entrepreneurs, and setting standards for local services by local organizations are two good examples.

- **Link Benefits to Conservation.** The links between ecotourism benefits and conservation objectives need to be direct and significant. Income, employment and other benefits must promote conservation.

- **Distribute Benefits.** Ensure that both the community and individuals benefit from projects.

- **Identify Community Leaders.** Identify opinion leaders and involve them in the planning and execution of projects. Identify leaders that represent different constituents to ensure that a cross-section of society is involved (including both men and women). Be sure the project has good information on the local social structure. Strategize on the effects of the projects on different social groups and never assume that all parts of society will cooperate or agree. Be strategic and gain appropriate allies early.

- **Bring About Change.** Use existing organizations already working in the community to improve its social well-being through economic development. Development associations or local cooperatives are good prospects. Groups involved in organizing recreation can also be good allies. Community participation through institutions is more likely to bring about effective and sustained change.

- **Understand Site-Specific Conditions.** Be aware that authority structures vary greatly in each region. Consensus is not always possible, nor is the full participation of all sectors of society (women are often excluded).

- **Monitor and Evaluate Progress.** Establish indicators in advance to track tourism's impacts – both positive and negative. Goals such as employment and income levels are only one type of indicator. The project should track negative impacts such as evidence of rapidly escalating prices for local goods, inflation in land prices, antagonism towards visitors, frequency of arrests, change in youth activities, and evidence of drug, prostitution and other illicit activities. Ideally, the more the local community is fully involved in ecotourism development, the less these problems should develop. Another important indicator of local involvement is evidence of initiatives within the community to respond to the negative influences of tourism.

Brandon, *Ecotourism: A Guide for Planners & Managers – Volume 1*, 1993

making structure but may instead decide by consensus. This can be very slow and painstaking. It also must be understood that if the community is not involved in initial decisions for the project – such as establishing the objectives for the project or defining its scope – they likely will care less about its success.

Ecotourism development procedures include reviewing with the community the range of possible project

Posadas Amazonas – A Case Study from Peru

In May 1996, the members of the local Native Community of Infierno (CNI) and a private Peruvian tour operator, Rain Forest Expeditions (RFE), signed a legally binding contract to build and co-manage a lodge called Posadas Amazonas. The partners agreed to split the profits 60% to the community, and 40% to the company, and to divide the management responsibilities in half. A critical tenet of the agreement was that community members should be actively involved in the enterprise, not only as staff, but also as owners, planners and administrators, and that they should join RFE in making decisions about the company's future. The partners also agreed that after 20 years, the lodge would belong to CNI. In return, the CNI members were obligated to maintain an exclusive contract with RFE on communal territory for 20 years.

In the project's first year, the community's participation was relatively passive. One of the obstacles to equal management participation was the community members' sheer lack of experience, and their uncertainty what full participation entailed. Only one year later, the community partners became more active decision makers. In general, the community members were more aware of their status and privilege as partners. For most in the community, this sense of ownership came only after the project was up and running, and after they had invested their own time in creating it. Members of the community now comment, "they have theories, but we have the experience." Learning has gone both ways. The staff of Rain Forest Expeditions changed considerably, learning to listen and leave more of the decisions to the community. They became more appreciative of local skills and traditional forms of organization and more attentive to voices that before remained unheard. At the same time, the members of CNI learned how to better forecast into the future, weighing advantages and disadvantages of various development options before proceeding with their next step.

Adapted from Stronza, *Because It Is Ours*, 2000

benefits (both economic and social) and its potential negative impacts. Using trained intermediaries skilled at community facilitation and assessment at this stage is highly recommended. All experts in community development agree that the community must have the information needed to decide if the project's negative impacts may outweigh the benefits, before proceeding with a new project. If the project is approved by the community, community representatives must be clearly integrated into the decision-making process during all phases of the project. A written agreement between the ecotourism project and the community can help to give both sides the security of having all roles and responsibilities clearly defined from the outset. As part of successful agreements, communities must have the means to invest in projects using the types of resources available to them, such as labor, local renewable resources and land. Case studies indicate that the community must invest in the project in order for it to be a success.

Local guide, Peru

Community-Based Ecotourism

Community-based ecotourism (CBE) is a growing phenomenon throughout the developing world. The CBE concept implies that the community has substantial control and involvement in the ecotourism project, and that the majority of benefits remain in the community. Three main types of CBE enterprises have been identified. The purest model suggests that the community owns and manages the enterprise. All community members are employed by the project using a rotation system, and profits are allocated to community projects. The second type of CBE enterprise involves family or group initiatives within communities. The third type of CBE is a joint venture between a community or family and an outside business partner.

Certainly all efforts should be made to maximize benefits to local communities, but it may not be realistic to expect that an entire community can control and manage ecotourism. Researchers Rolf

Wesche and Andy Drumm comment in their 1999 book *Defending Our Rain Forest: A Guide to Community-Based Ecotourism in the Ecuadorian Amazon* that "the notion of long-term communal enterprise requires the permanent, consistent

---

A Community-Based Ecotourism Experience – The Traveler's Perspective

Tourists are greeted by community leaders and stay in village guest houses that are simple in design and similar to other houses in the community. Locals take tourists for hikes to natural sites and tell them about the traditional uses of resources in the area. Traditional stories about natural sites are often shared. Tourists are given a chance to learn about how the local community perceives its natural setting, their wildlife and wild lands, and to learn something about local customs. After a full day outdoors, tourists are treated to local cooking and have an option to buy handicrafts from villagers. Evening gatherings take place in community houses or centers, where an exchange of worldviews takes place between hosts and guests. This can lead to long-lasting bonds between community members and their visitors.

Behind the Scenes of a CBE Experience – The Community Perspective

The local community typically organizes itself to manage tourism by establishing a cooperative or small company with community shareholders. Homestays often are rotated between community members to ensure all families have the opportunity to host tourists. While a leader must emerge to manage the tourism enterprise, the input and involvement of the whole community is essential for success. Younger community members often take a keener interest in leading the enterprise, while older members prefer to maintain their traditional lifestyles of hunting or farming. Conflicts and questions may arise about the old versus new way of life, but unique relationships emerge when the young managers work together with their elders to teach tourists about medicinal plants and other traditional uses of the natural resources.

Previously disinterested youth may seek to increase their traditional knowledge for tourist guiding and may do so by approaching their shamans or other traditional leaders. Home-based craft making is often revived, with women using ancient and at times abandoned craft techniques to increase the value of their products. Extended networks of women may form crafts cooperatives. These cooperatives provide important empowerment centers for women who work together to sell a wide variety of distinctive products in one central location. This type of commerce frequently gives women new independence and more clout in their own households. Frequently women will speak out against such destructive trends as abuse and alcoholism, once they have the economic independence they need.

The keys to success are community control over the tourist product and management through community discussion that addresses any concerns over tourism management. Transparent accounting practices are vital to equitably share the economic benefits with all members of the community.

Community women with new product, Mexico

While CBE projects remain an evolving framework for tourism development, they are not a utopian concept. Wesche and Drumm documented more than 30 CBE projects in the Ecuadorian Amazon alone, based on the definitions supplied above. While there are variations, the descriptions on page 41 of the CBE experience are based on dozens of actual experiences in Latin America.

While the CBE concept is less studied in regions outside Latin America, an Overseas Development Institute study looked at CBE projects in Namibia, described below.

commitment of all community members. It has to be learned and reinforced through positive experience. Problems have resulted from the communal enterprise approach such as the slowness of democratic decision making and inconsistent quality of services. The community enterprise model is being adapted to allow for allocation of responsibilities to specialized, trained members of the community."

Women and Ecotourism

A wide range of studies on rural development demonstrate that women are less likely to benefit from development initiatives than men, unless special measures are taken to involve them. This problem prevails in ecotourism development projects as well. A study on gender issues and tourism in Indonesia

Community-Based Ecotourism – A Case Study from Namibia

Residents of Namibia are forming conservancies which under law gives them conditional use rights over wildlife. Nearly all the four registered conservancies and more than a dozen emerging conservancies are actively developing tourism plans and have become key actors in rural tourism development.

Residents of the Bergsig area formed the Torra Conservancy, which became involved with two different tourism investors. The residents selected a small camp-style proposal over a potentially more lucrative lodge proposal because the proposed luxury lodge would have impinged on the local way of life, including livestock management and access to water sources. The community selected the camp because it was small-scale, required a lease for only 10 years and, importantly, the campground operator had established a high level of trust within the community. NGOs were identified as important resources that guided the community, outlined the benefits and pointed out the disadvantages of incorporating tourism into community life.

The government in Namibia presently recognizes community tourism enterprises, rural residents and the emerging conservancies as significant players in tourism. Current regional tourism planning procedures include considerable community consultation. In addition, community tourism enterprises in Namibia have joined forces to form the Namibian Community Based Tourism Association, which is recognized by government and consulted on many matters.

Ashley, *The Impact of Tourism on Rural Livelihoods*, 2000

Weaver selling wares, Peru

(*Shah & Gupta 2000*) shows that women were willing to increase their workloads tremendously through the sale of handicrafts, in order to gain some new measure of financial independence.

Programs to involve women in ecotourism development are still scarce. One good example of such a program is in Nepal, undertaken by the Mountain Institute (*see below*).

Langtang Ecotourism Project –A Case Study from Nepal

Women in Nepal have lower literacy rates, educational opportunities, access to resources, control of assets and decision-making powers than men. For many women the tasks of caring for tourists adds considerably to their daily household duties, especially when husbands are away working as trekking porters and guides. They are never idle, however – whatever time they have to sit down is spent knitting woolen caps, mittens and socks, weaving bags, or making handicrafts for sale. Much attention is paid in Nepal to gender issues, but real progress has been rare.

The Langtang Ecotourism Project was established in 1996 to build local capacity for tourism management. Women embraced the program and played a vital role in the transition from trying to meet tourism demand to proactively developing sustainably managed tourist services. Through a special participatory planning approach, they developed a collective dream of how community-based tourism could look and function in the future. For example, by participating in the assessment of different cooking fuels, they elected to use kerosene instead of wood. A kerosene depot was established and the profits are now allocated to conservation initiatives, such as the planting of 17,500 tree seedlings. Independent of becoming local environmental managers, the women also have coordinated a cultural revival. Craft cooperatives, traditional dancing and singing are now generating income for the women of the community and promoting pride in their local culture.

Adapted from Brewer-Lama, *Cultural Survival Quarterly*, 1999

Mutawintji National Park – A Case Study from Australia

Mutawintji has been a popular tourist destination in New South Wales (NSW), Australia, since the 1880s because of its famous gorges, rock pools and Aboriginal rock art. The NSW Parks and Wildlife Service opened a campground there in the 1970s without any involvement of Aboriginal people. By the 1980s, Aboriginal people were so outraged by unregulated tourist behavior that they blockaded the park to control the area and demand respect for their sacred sites. In 1996, the parliament of New South Wales passed legislation that enabled the return of ownership of several national parks to their traditional Aboriginal owners using "joint management" agreements with the NSW National Parks and Wildlife Service. These agreements were to be overseen by boards with a majority of traditional owners. Mutawintji National Park became the first park returned to its Aboriginal owners as agreed by parliament.

A Mutawintji Local Aboriginal Land Council (MLALC) is now in charge of all tours in the park, and members of the council handle all guided tours. The MLALC has formally licensed its own tour operation, Mutawintji Heritage Tours, which serves as a liaison with all non-indigenous tour operators on behalf of the park. The enterprise received federal funding for guide training, which has taken place, resulting in improved skills and confidence among Aboriginal guides. The company is steadily aiming for self sufficiency, and plans to be free of the need for further funding in a few years. General satisfaction with tourism management in the area has improved considerably since 1996.

Adapted from Sutton, *Cultural Survival Quarterly*, 1999

Ecotourism and Indigenous Communities

Ecotourism may often be identified as a means by which communities can raise their standard of living without unsustainable exploitation of natural resources or cultural degradation. Indigenous communities have very special opportunities to develop ecotourism, because they often live in remote natural areas. However, ecotourism is not necessarily the proper course for indigenous communities. Most indigenous people have been marginalized by their national governments. Frequently they do not have land rights, giving them little clout or control over the development of their homelands. Furthermore, they may be subject to a number of pressures to change their social, technological and even religious practices to adopt a market- or service-based economy. This can lead to highly unjust situations where tourism is developed without permission on their own lands.

The relationship between indigenous communities and tourism has long been tenuous. Tourism businesses have frequently used local resources with little economic benefit to the community. If local people were involved in tourism, it was as cheap labor or as part of the tourist attraction, mostly in the form of cultural "shows" or displays. This problem continues today, giving indigenous people a natural distrust of tourism development in general, and little reason to believe in the potential of ecotourism. They often perceive it as just one more proposal to eliminate local control over their land and their community's future – and, unfortunately, their concerns may be justified in many instances.

An indigenous working group at a Side-Event at the 2000 Conference of Parties to the Convention on Biological Diversity in Nairobi summarized some of the indigenous community's key concerns. Their points included:

1. The need for tools to ensure prior informed consent;
2. The need to undertake a collective review of prior informed consent;
3. The need to determine criteria for cultural diversity within the context of biological diversity;
4. The creation of a process for grievances and conflict resolutions for indigenous peoples;
5. Development of a deeper appreciation for indigenous rights separate from rural communities and others.

Some indigenous people have been able to take full control of tourism development, while other groups have entered co-management agreements that provide them with a measure of control to protect their land rights, prevent desecration of sacred areas, and reap economic benefits from tourism without undermining their cultural identity. This process cannot proceed successfully unless the indigenous community has legal control over land and full legal rights to protect any businesses that they may establish. If these vital elements are in place, an indigenous community is in the position to take advantage of ecotourism and use it as a sustainable development tool.

Efforts to make ecotourism fully beneficial to local communities are still very new and often experimental. Some communities around the world are keen to get involved, but assistance will be needed to gauge their market potential and real-life business opportunities before development projects are initiated. Certainly communities need their voices heard, and they need to be given the opportunity to develop the skills to fully participate in ecotourism development. Sustained efforts to involve local communities will be required to ensure they are fully

part of this international market, when they choose to be.

Regional and National Governments

Governments have an extraordinarily important role to play in the development of ecotourism, yet their role is complex and must be defined by a variety of agency players. Several countries have adopted specific ecotourism strategies. The first national ecotourism plan in the world, prepared by the Australian government in 1994, is the most important example of national ecotourism planning. The government of Brazil also published *Guidelines for an Ecotourism National Policy* (*Grupo de Trabalho Interministerial, 1994*), which set a benchmark for action in that nation. These plans have a strong focus on the development of appropriate tourism infrastructure and capabilities for the development of tourism in natural areas with a high level of commitment to rural peoples, making them classic examples of ecotourism planning. The commitment to national ecotourism planning development in Australia and Brazil has been very strong because these countries recognized that their tourism economies depend upon the health of their natural ecosystems.

Australia

In Australia, the decision to formulate an ecotourism strategy was made in response to growing international interest and the increasing profile of Australia's natural environment as a tourism attraction. Working on behalf of the federal government, a small team undertook a literature review and proceeded to public consultation, which involved local government agencies, natural resource managers, tour operators, tourism marketers, planners, conservation and community groups, developers and indigenous Australians. Workshops were convened around

Australian National Ecotourism Strategy

Challenges

1. Maintain acceptable levels of visitor use.
2. Adopt minimum impact practices.
3. Use monitoring to maintain oversight on resource impact.

Objectives

1. Facilitate ecologically sustainable practices.
2. Integrate regional planning.
   a. Urge local participation in the planning and decision-making process.
   b. Improve use of biophysical parameters in permitting process.
3. Improve natural resource management.
   a. Seek financial benefits from entrance and permit fees.
   b. Review permitting for use by operators.
4. Improve cooperation between ecotourism and natural resource management.
   a. Specify mode of transport, points of entry, licensing and permits.
   b. Train site-specific operators in ecologically sustainable practices.
5. Provide proper regulations.
   a. Study environmental impacts of tourism developments in natural areas.
   b. Develop guidelines or codes of practice for private sector.
   c. Accredit private sector.
   d. Remove inconsistencies between regional, state and territorial licensing and zoning regulations.
6. Determine infrastructure needs.
   a. Increase capability to withstand environmental impacts.
   b. Disperse crowds by directing flow of tourists to sites.
   c. Offer educational information.
   d. Provide site-sensitive design.
   e. Utilize environmentally-friendly waste management and energy systems.
7. Monitor visitor impacts.
   a. Establish baseline data on sites.
8. Develop information base.
   a. Develop database on cultural and ecotourism attractions.
   b. Develop database on existing operators servicing these attractions.
9. Conduct marketing.
   a. Gather data on the market niches attracted to specific destinations.
   b. Create market profiles for destinations.
10. Deliver ethical ecotourism products.
    a. Develop local industry standards.
    b. Accredit ecotourism products.
11. Enhance opportunities for self-determination.
    a. Enhance abilities of local people to manage destinations.
    b. Enhance abilities of Aboriginal peoples to self-sufficiently manage sites.
12. Develop business policies.
    a. Offer opportunities sensitive to ecotourism business needs.

Commonwealth of Australia, *National Ecotourism Strategy*, 1994

Ecolodge in Amazon, Brazil

the country, and a call for written submissions was placed in the national press. According to Jill Grant and Alison Allcock, the two co-authors of Australia's national plan, "it was the consultative process that inspired and stimulated the direction of the document."

The final objectives for the National Strategy are outlined on page 46.

Brazil

Ecotourism began in Brazil as a small market niche driven by the demand for school field trips focusing on environmental studies. This changed, however, when international visitation began to rapidly increase – until 1994, Brazil received less than 2 million international visitors annually, but by 1998 this figure reached 5 million people annually and was increasing. To address the environmental threat of rapid tourism growth, the Brazilian government established the Interministerial Ecotourism Task Force in the early 1990s. This group produced *Guidelines for an Ecotourism National Policy*, which was officially endorsed and released by President Fernando Henrique Cardoso in March 1995.

The Ministry of the Environment took the lead in implementing the ecotourism policy guidelines. Nine Amazon states were used to test the guidelines due to the high biodiversity value and growing tourist demand to see the Amazon rain forest. Efforts to protect the rich biological heritage of the Brazilian Amazon, which is roughly 5 million square kilometers in size, have been hampered by its vast size and remoteness. Protected areas cover just 3.2% of the region, and the parks are in scattered, hard-to-reach locations, all understaffed and without management plans or infrastructure to allow visitation. At present the average stay of a tourist in Amazonian Brazil is just 3.5 days because of its remoteness, lack of infrastructure, and lack of qualified ecotourism businesses in the region capable of giving visitors a true sense of its wonders.

A technical cooperation program was developed for the Amazon region and signed in 2000 by President Cardoso. The Inter-American Development Bank (IDB) loaned US$13.8 million to establish a framework to implement the necessary investments in the nine Brazilian Amazonian states to responsibly prepare

Starting Points for Government Ecotourism Programs

- Establish an Inter-Ministerial Working Group that combines expertise of Ministries of Tourism, Environment and the agency or agencies charged with rural development, natural resources or park authority.
- Empower and fund a secretariat of experts that work in the fields of natural resource management, community development and tourism.
- Develop a participatory planning program that involves stakeholders from throughout the country or region, including rural and indigenous communities.
- Establish objectives for a program based on stakeholder input, such as increased rural economic development, increased budgets for management of protected areas, and better management of visitors in fragile areas.
- Review transportation corridors, trail systems, small-scale non-commercial river transportation systems, small aircraft access and other infrastructure necessary to develop ecotourism. Develop a transportation plan that facilitates good ecotourism itineraries; stresses low environmental impact, low energy use, visitor safety and scenic qualities; and provides quality visitor information.
- Develop both policies to meet objectives and budgetary mechanisms to fund them. Seek legislative approvals where necessary.
- Develop a visitor information program and niche marketing plan.
- Develop a long-term community training program to develop community participation in ecotourism development.
- Establish biological and social carrying capacity benchmarks through research that establishes long-term monitoring of tourism impacts.
- Develop finance mechanisms for the development of small ecolodges, which provide incentives to conserve land and train local people.
- Develop an information base and best practice information through university research programs on issues of ethical delivery of ecotourism products, certification and visitor management plans.
- Develop land-use planning capacity in local municipalities through exposure to the benefits of zoning and regulatory techniques. Limit dense development in buffer zones of protected lands and other important ecotourism attractions.

themselves to manage selected ecotourism areas. This loan package, called Proecotur, is a pre-investment for a major effort to develop the country's Amazon region for ecotourism. The pre-investment stage will proceed by having all nine Amazonian states develop ecotourism strategies, including the following measures:

1. Strengthen the legal framework of these regions to regulate tourist activities.
2. Prepare a detailed market study.
3. Develop 19 management plans for existing and newly established protected areas.
4. Make key pilot investments in ecotourism products and sites.
5. Prepare 19 pre-feasibility and feasibility studies for infrastructure projects.
6. Implement training and capacity-building programs throughout the region.
7. Create a website to inform the public on the project's progress.

Government Planning Guidelines

Because ecotourism is a growing market, governments around the world are expressing increasing interest in attracting it as part of their tourism development program. While no guidelines for government planning of ecotourism exist, the above box provides a set of starting points.

Development Agencies

Multilateral development agencies, such as World Bank, European Commission and InterAmerican Development Bank (IDB), as well as bilateral agencies including the United Kingdom's Department for International Development (DFID), U.S. Agency for International Development (USAID), German Ministry for Economic Development (GTZ), Norwegian Agency for Development Cooperation (NORAD) and Canadian International Development Agency (CIDA), have become increasingly involved in funding ecotourism projects with loans and grants. Most of these organizations have strict guidelines that target the alleviation of poverty and, in the past, this has kept development agencies and banks out of tourism development work. Since the early 1990s, an ever-increasing number of development agency projects have been addressing environmental deterioration and the loss of biological diversity. Small portions of these projects have allocated funding to alternative sustainable development initiatives, such as ecotourism.

At present, development agencies fund ecotourism development in the following ways:

1. Through programs that offer conciliatory loan rates to "green" businesses in developing countries.
2. Through programs that offer loans to developing nations for the development of tourism as an important source of foreign exchange, with the understanding that tourism must be developed according to strict environmental and social guidelines.
3. Through loans, such as Proecotur in Brazil, that seek to use sustainable development of an under-developed region to contribute to the protection of biological diversity of critical ecosystems, such as the Brazilian Amazon.
4. Through grant programs that assist the development of micro-enterprises.
5. Through grant programs that assist the conservation of biological diversity and protected area management.

For the most part, ecotourism is not identified as a funding priority by development agencies, and it is difficult to find it when searching their funding records because it falls under larger categories of development assistance. Because it is such a new category of assistance, few development agencies have specified policies for ecotourism to date.

GTZ's manual *Tourism in Technical Cooperation* (*Steck* et al *1999*) provides policy approaches

---

Procedures Necessary in First Stage of Ecotourism Technical Assistance

- Examine national tourism strategies.
- Examine laws and regulations in force, e.g. regulations on land ownership, land utilization rights, conditions and controls for authorizing tourism facilities and infrastructural measures, regulation of investment incentives, etc.
- Introduce the collection of statistical data to gauge the development of ecotourism.
- Improve cross-sector coordination, especially between institutions of tourism and environment and nature conservation agencies.
- Create new or adapt existing national image and marketing programs as a by-product of the strategic goals of the sustainable development of ecotourism.
- Create/consolidate the legal framework for local authorities or NGOs to actively participate in cooperative protected area management as well as generate and manage their own revenues from tourism.
- Create inter-regional and inter-communal benefit and financial adjustment mechanisms to avoid or reduce disparities brought about by tourism development.

Steck et al, *Tourism in Technical Cooperation*, 1999

for technical assistance in ecotourism. Other agencies seeking to develop loan and grant programs can use this model to produce good projects with conservation outcomes and measurable benefits to local communities. One key set of recommendations is supplied here.

European and American researchers followed up on the work done by GTZ by holding an *Ecotourism Development Policy Forum* at IDB in Washington, D.C., in September 1999, co-sponsored by The International Ecotourism Society, Conservation International, World Resources Institute and Environmental Enterprises Assistance Fund. Meeting participants wanted to ensure a productive funding environment for ecotourism, to structure successful ecotourism finance packages, to set criteria for funding projects, and to energize cooperation between equity investors, donors and green loan funds. Results from this meeting are in draft form (*see next column*).

European researchers (*SECA 2000*) involved in the 1999 IDB meeting subsequently undertook research for France's Global Environmental Facility on ecotourism development policy. They found that ecotourism is of increasing interest to European development agencies, but that assistance is usually part of larger projects. DFID's Tourism Challenge Fund, which was established to provide small focused grants to projects where the private sector is working with communities, is the one assistance program in Europe that specifically targets ecotourism as a fundable item. Researchers found that most agencies support projects that seek to link biodiversity conservation with poverty reduction within local communities, local culture preservation, sensitive promotion to visitors, and biodiversity improvements. Researchers also found that strict criteria and evaluation procedures are rare and that only informal principals and approaches for funding have been identified.

Draft results from the 1999 IDB meeting prepared by The International Ecotourism Society and Conservation International found the following:

1. Critical gaps exist in knowledge and information regarding ecotourism.
2. No brokering entity is currently available that can bring effective ecotourism projects to the point where loan funds are effective.
3. Government tourism agencies lack knowledge on how to develop appropriate packages for donor agencies.
4. Ecotourism projects in the donor community lack coordination and have high overlap.
5. Donor packages intended to conserve biological diversity often have failed to properly account for tourism market realities.

Draft recommendations from the 1999 Ecotourism Development Policy Forum follow:

1. Establish an ecotourism consultative group that joins representatives of NGOs, multilaterals and bilaterals with expert country representatives.
2. Create a grant-funded "deal-making" entity that could incubate good ecotourism business projects and broker them.
3. Test an innovative combination of loan and grant funds to ensure that biodiversity and social impact studies are undertaken and that long-term monitoring and evaluation take place.

In summary, it is clear that new innovative policies for ecotourism are needed to ensure that technical assistance meets the demand for serious long-term projects that are sustainable and fully prepared to compete in the market. The 1999 IDB meeting also indicated that traditional finance mechanisms demand rates of return that are well above what standard ecotourism projects can offer, and that grant mechanisms should fully fund the complex systems and programs required to make ecotourism sustainable.

Developing the Capacity for Successful Ecotourism

Research Community

Research is crucial to minimize the impacts of ecotourism in natural areas and to build technical capabilities that manage and deliver quality ecotourism. Universities play a critical role in ecotourism development by offering technical support in the form of both academic research and documentation of best practice case studies.

The Australian government identified a range of areas where ecotourism research was needed and worked with the university community to develop a better base of information. This was put into practice via the National Ecotourism Program (NEP), which made competitive grants available:

NEP identified four central research themes that were pivotal to the development of Australia's ecotourism industry:

Australian National Ecotourism Program Research

- **Energy and Waste Minimization Study:** A comprehensive investigation of how the private sector could implement sustainable energy practices and benefit by minimizing their waste stream.
- **Ecotourism Education Consultancy:** A study of current and future education and training needs of the ecotourism industry, and the creation of a directory of training courses, education resource materials and useful contacts.
- **Business Development Consultancy:** An investigation of the networks and alliances needed for cooperative marketing, purchasing and skill sharing.
- **Market Research Consultancy:** A market profile of ecotourists, their expectations and interests.

Grant, Allcock, 1998.

The research program's results provided guidance on many issues for ecotourism developers. For example, the Australian federal government in 1994 published *A Guide to Innovative Technology for Sustainable Tourism*, followed one year later by *Best Practice Ecotourism: A Guide to Energy and Waste Minimization*. Both publications, developed with NEP research grants, concluded that the greatest measurable negative impact of tourism stems from excessive use of natural resources and the production of waste. The researchers recommended that the ecotourism industry, like the rest of the tourism industry, address these issues. To provide guidance to the fledgling ecotourism

---

Australian National Ecotourism Program Grant Guidelines

- **Infrastructure development:** Projects that utilize innovative designs and technologies, and environmental protection approaches such as boardwalks and wildlife viewing platforms.
- **Baseline studies and monitoring:** Projects that assess the impact of tourist infrastructure on environmental processes.
- **Regional ecotourism planning:** Projects that encourage local participation in planning and decision-making.

Grant, Allcock, 1998.

---

industry, these studies provided concrete examples of how new technologies and practices could be adopted to achieve more ecologically and socially sustainable outcomes. The grants established collaborative networks that continue to exist today such as the Ecotourism Association of Australia.

To address the long-term research goals of the tourism industry, the Cooperative Research Center for Sustainable Tourism was founded in 1997 in Australia with A$14.72 million of government funds. The CRC researches numerous aspects of sustainable tourism,

Limits of Acceptable Change – A Research Case Study from the United States

Since the 1970s, the overwhelming growth of recreation in U.S. protected areas was leading to damage of fragile natural resources. To cope with the problem, the U.S. federal government sponsored research using the state university cooperative research program, which had already worked with federal agency resource managers for decades on land management and wildlife conservation issues.

The concept of carrying capacity emerged from the biological sciences to take on a new meaning in the field of tourism. Today the tourist carrying capacity is defined as the level of human activity an area can accommodate without adverse effects on the natural environment, resident community or on the quality of visitor experience. During the 1970s and 1980s, the U.S. Forest Service developed a model to address carrying capacity for tourism management in protected areas and in 1985 released *The Limits of Acceptable Change (LAC) System for Wilderness Planning* (Stankey et al, 1985).

The principles behind LAC had been developed by many researchers over the years, but this publication summed up much of the relevant work, and gave it a new focus by establishing measurable impact benchmarks that are identified and reviewed periodically in a public consultation process. New systems have been formulated over the years, but LAC is still the landmark system by which all others are measured. Today the money spent by the American government some decades ago helps protect U.S. public lands and many protected area systems throughout the world.

Guide Training Guidelines – A Research Case Study on Capacity Building

- Select an appropriate group of course participants to implement ecotourism's principles in the field.
- Teaching and learning should be collaborative and interesting. Short lectures and many small group activities are needed to improve understanding of concepts.
- Trainees should be encouraged to learn and perform at their own level; educators need to recognize different learning styles and teach appropriately.
- Programs should be cost effective to enable the best candidates to attend, not just the wealthiest.
- Training the trainer should be a priority in developing nations where outside expertise comes at considerable cost sacrifice; local training maximizes the benefits to the host economy.
- Training requests should come from the host country, not from foreign intermediaries.

Adapted from Weiler and Ham, *New Frontiers in Tourism Research*, 1999

including ecotourism, and is focused on practical solutions. It is facilitated through private partners and a variety of university and other research institutions.

Research also played a key role in developing visitor management systems for national parks in the United States. Ffforts to develop better processes fell to universities in the U.S. that traditionally worked with land management agencies such as the U.S. Forest Service and U.S. Park Service. These systems have been extensively adapted by protected land managers and ecotourism projects around the world (*see* Limits of Acceptable Change Case Study *page 52*).

Another critical research area has been the development of techniques to improve field guides' capacity to properly convey information to ecotourists in a manner that is both accurate and engaging. Researchers Betty Weiler and Sam Ham, experts in field interpretation, have evaluated guide training strategies in many developing countries, with conclusions in the box on page 52.

Because ecotourism is still an emerging field, the research community provides an invaluable resource to governments that are developing policies. Using funds for research can help address difficult management issues and avoid many potential mistakes. Researchers can quickly assess management approaches for a particular site by gathering materials on what has been tested and implemented successfully throughout the world. Before establishing policies of any kind, it is of paramount importance that research be used as the basis for real solutions.

Interpretive guide, Australia

Non-Governmental Organizations

Non-governmental organizations are critical players in developing ecotourism's capacity worldwide. Some of the projects undertaken by NGOs include:

1. Training and capacity building initiatives, particularly for communities, that stress guiding skills, language and small enterprise development.
2. Establishing standards and guiding the development of ethical business standards through stakeholder meetings and forums.
3. Management of ecotourism certification programs.
4. Training young entrepreneurs worldwide on principles involved in managing responsible businesses.
5. Working with governments and international agencies to develop sustainable ecotourism policies.
6. Working with protected area agencies to establish visitor management capacity.

7. Representing underrepresented communities, such as indigenous people who at times lack political and social rights, in policy dialogues.

Non-governmental organizations are able to assess how to improve the benefits from ecotourism and establish their objectives based on who needs assistance. International and local NGOs frequently partner to design and develop projects that will enhance local capacity for higher levels of sustainability (*see below*). With the help of foundations and development agency funding, NGOs have significant influence on ecotourism development policies and programs, and also are important watchdogs for inappropriate policies.

Ecotourism Training Program – An NGO Case Study

RARE Center for Tropical Conservation developed its guide training program in 1994 to develop basic skills for guiding and operating tours in Costa Rica. RARE's goal was to offer residents an economically viable alternative to unsustainable livelihoods via the growing industry of ecotourism. The guide training courses have since been extended to Mexico and Honduras, and courses are being planned for South Africa.

The Nature Guide Training Program was developed collaboratively between protected area managers, local tour operators and Worldteach (a Harvard University-based volunteer organization). Students live and study in an English-only environment for three months and receive more than 1,000 hours of practical experience (equivalent to more than a year at a U.S. university). The program is based on experiential learning; students design and lead tours as well as examine the inter-related components of tourism, from signage to product marketing.

To date, RARE's Nature Guide Training Program has conducted 12 workshops and graduated 180 participants. On average, graduates earn 92% more than before the course, adding additional revenue of more than $1 million locally. From the Baja California Sur program, 65% of participants work as nature guides, while another 18% work or study in conservation or ecotourism-related activities. In Mexico, 76% of students are guiding while more than a dozen have launched ecotourism businesses in their communities. These graduates also run community programs that have educated more than 500 local adults and children.

Conclusion

Ecotourism has proven itself to be an important tool for conservation, and in certain cases it has improved the quality of life of local people, who continue to demand it as a sustainable development option. But its record has been far from uniform throughout the world. Evaluating ecotourism as a global sustainable development tool is a difficult task. It has been frequently mislabeled and implemented in ways that do not meet the standards articulated in this document. Each region of the world and their local communities will have to decide for themselves what is appropriate.

In order to become a successful sustainable development tool worldwide, ecotourism requires a thorough investigation into the planning of ecotourism destinations and their long-term management – and adequate government funds must be made available for this. Budgets need to properly acknowledge the important role of conserving areas, both cultural and environmental, for ecotourism development. Specialized fees and taxes need to be channeled into resource protection and visitor management. Clearly no destination will prosper in the long-term – particularly an eco-destination – if it is not properly managed to prevent overcrowding, environmental impacts and the loss of its biological and cultural integrity.

It is time to initiate better policies that reinvest the revenues generated by tourism into proper tourism planning and management. Tourism ministries need to take a place at the national economic planning table with other ministries. Tourism policies must stress a quality visitor experience and site integrity, not just marketing and high visitor numbers. New economic indicators are needed to determine what kind of tourism development is most economically and socially beneficial to the nation, and environmental policies must be put in place, particularly land-use planning. Tourism management is developing into a refined science and a field of excellence. The use of research and technological tools, such as Geographic Information Systems and satellite imagery, will make it easier to create appropriate tourist zones and regulations.

On the other hand, community involvement and benefits must become a requirement from the inception of all ecotourism projects. While some outstanding small-scale private sector projects have made communities their full partners, and some good examples of community-based ecotourism exist, each new project struggles to develop itself appropriately, rarely benefiting from the experience of others. While every success story is different, governments and NGOs must recognize that community ecotourism

Ecotourism project partners, Mexico

development must have long-term support; short-term projects simply will not suffice. Mechanisms that ensure a degree of local control and equitable community-wide benefit distribution have to be available and implemented.

Achieving genuine ecotourism may be viewed either as a difficult technical challenge or an impossible task. Some observe that those who hold the reins of power and money will always prevail, and that ecotourism will never genuinely offer benefits to local people. While this may be true in many circumstances, this same viewpoint has validity no matter what type of development is being discussed. Similar to other types of development, ecotourism offers opportunities, but it can never provide an entire solution. The solution must come from a will of all involved to achieve sustainable results.

Ecotourism Hosts and Guests

As more come to know and love our planet, conservation of its natural resources will become a passion for an ever-growing percentage of the world's population. Ecotourism can and will be a tremendous contributor to the education of international travelers, as well as to the growing global middle class who are traveling in their own countries, and local people who are hosting ecotourists. The opportunity for a genuine exchange of environmental values between travelers and their hosts and the rediscovery of the importance of traditions that value a destination's land and spirit cannot be undervalued.

Not all will choose to take part in this interchange between peoples. And communities must have the power to choose their own fate. However, many people desire to communicate between cultures, host guests from outside their home region, and learn from one another.

A huge majority of the planet's population now resides in urban areas. If the future of the planet depends on humankind's commitment to conserve its environment, then surely ecotourism has a role to play. If the underlying principles of ecotourism are increasingly embraced, more people will visit natural areas with an understanding of what they are seeing and experiencing. Ecotourism is a sustainable development tool that regularly creates contact between people on opposite sides of the earth, as hosts and guests. If an ecotourism experience can truly reach the hearts and minds of both – convincing them that efforts to help conserve the environment can make a difference – the chances of achieving conservation and sustainable development into the next millennium are a little bit greater.

Resource Documents

Alderman, C. L.1990. A Study of the role of Privately Owned Lands Used for Nature Tourism, Education and Conservation, Washington D.C., USA.

ARA Consulting Group Inc. and HLA Consultants 1994, *Ecotourism-Nature Adventure I Culture: Alberta and British Columbia Market Demand Assessment*, Vancouver, British Columbia, Canada.

Ashley, C. 2000, Working Paper: *The Impact of Tourism on Rural Livelihoods, Namibia's Experience*, Overseas Development Institute, UK.

Baez, A.L. and Fernandez, L., 1994, *Ecoutourism as an economic activity: The case of Tortuguero in Costa Rica*. A paper presented at the First World Conference of Tourism and Environment in Belize.

Ballantine, B. and Eagles, P. 1994, 'Defining Canadian Ecotourists, *Journal of Sustainable Tourism*, 2 (4): 210-214.

Bermúdez, F. 1992, *Evolución del Turismo en las áreas silvestres*, Servicio de Parques Nacionales, Costa Rica.

Blamey, R. and Hatch, D. 1998, *Profiles and Motivations of Nature-based Tourists Visiting Australia: Occasional Paper Number 25*, Bureau of Tourism Research, Canberra, Australia.

Blangy, S. and Vautier, S., 2001, 'Europe', in Weaver, D. (ed.), *The Encyclopedia of Ecotourism*, CAB International, Oxon, UK.

Boo, E. 1990, *Ecotourism: The Potentials and Pitfalls Vols. I & 2*, World Wildlife Fund, Washington, D.C., USA.

Brandon, K. 1993, 'Basic steps toward encouraging local participation in nature tourism projects' in: Lindberg, K. and Hawkins, D. (eds.), *Ecotourism: A guide for planners and managers,*

Volume 1, The International Ecotourism Society, Burlington, VT, USA.

Brewer Lama, W. 1999, 'Valuing women as assets to community-based tourism in Nepal', *Cultural Survival Quarterly, Vol.* 23, No.2, pp. 45 – 47, Cultural Survival, Cambridge, MA, USA.

Buckley, R. 2001, 'Ecotourism Accreditation in Australia', in: Font, X. and Buckley, R. (eds.),

Ecolabels in tourism: certification and promotion of sustainable management, CAB International, Wallingford, UK.

Caalders, J., van der Duim, R., Boon, G. and Quesada Rivel, H. *1999, Tourism and biodiversity: Impacts and perspectives on interventions in the Netherlands and Costa Rica*, Buiten Consultancy, The Netherlands.

Cater, E. and Lowman, G. (eds.) 1994, *Ecotourism: A Sustainable Option?*, John Wiley and Sons, Chichester, UK.

Ceballos Lascurain, H. 1996, *Tourism, ecotourism and protected areas, IUCN*, Gland, Switzerland.

Commonwealth Department of Tourism 1994, *A Guide to Innovative Technology for Sustainable Tourism*, Commonwealth of Australia, Canberra, Australia.

Commonwealth Department of Tourism 1994, *National Ecotourism Strategy*, Commonwealth of Australia, Canberra, Australia.

Commonwealth Department of Tourism 1995, *Best Practice Ecotourism: A Guide to Energy and Waste Minimisation*, Commonwealth of Australia, Canberra, Australia.

De Lacy, T. and Boyd, M. 2000, 'An Australian research partnership between industry, universities and government: The Cooperative

Research Centre for Sustainable Tourism' in: Bramwell, B. and Lane, B. (eds.), *Tourism Collaboration and Partnership: Politics, practice and sustainability*, Channel View Publications, Clevedon, UK.

Eagles, P. and Cascagnette, J. 1992, 'Canadian Ecotourists: Who Are They?', a paper presented at *Fourth Symposium on Social Science in Resources Management*, University of Wisconsin, Madison, Wisconsin, USA.

Eagles, P. and Higgins, B. 1998, 'New Directions in the Ecotourism Industry' in: Lindberg, K., Epler Wood, M. and Engeldrum, D. (eds.), *Ecotourism: A guide for planners and managers Volume 2*, The International Ecotourism Society, Burlington, VT, USA.

Epler Wood, M. 1997, *Ecotourism at a crossroads: Charting the way forward*, The International Ecotourism Society, Burlington, VT, USA.

Epler Wood, M. 1998, *Making the Global Challenge of Community Participation in Ecotourism: Case Studies & Lessons from Ecuador*, The Nature Conservancy, Washington D.C., USA.

Epler Wood, M. 1998, 'New Directions in the Ecotourism Industry' in: Lindberg, K., Epler Wood, M. and Engeldrum, D. (eds.), *Ecotourism: A guide for planners and managers Volume 2*, The International Ecotourism Society, Burlington, VT, USA.

Epler Wood, M. and Halpenny, E. 2001, 'Ecotourism certification and evaluation: progress and prospects' in: Font, X. and Buckley, R. (eds.), *Ecolabels in tourism: certification and promotion of sustainable management*, CAB International, Wallingford, UK.

Fillion, F., Foley, J. and Jacquemot, A. 1992, 'The Economics of Global Ecotourism', a paper presented at the Forth World Congress on National

Parks and Protected Areas, 10-21 February, Caracas, Venezuela.

Godde, P., Price, M. and Zimmermann, F. (eds.) 2000, *Tourism and Development in Mountain Regions,* CAB International, Oxon, UK.

Goodwin, H.J., Kent, I.J., Parker, K.T. and Walpole, M.J., 1997, *Tourism, Conservation & Sustainable Developpment, vol. I-IV, Final Report to the Department for Internaional Development,* Durrell Institute of Conservation and Ecology, University of Kent, U.K.

Grant, J. and Allcock, A. 1998, 'National planning limitations, objectives and lessons: The development of Australia's National Ecotourism Strategy', in: Lindberg, K., Epler Wood, M. and Engeldrum, D. (eds.), *Ecotourism: A guide for planners and managers Volume 2,* The International Ecotourism Society, Burlington, VT, USA.

Grupo de Trabalho Interministerial MICT 1994, *Diretrizes para uma politica nacional de ecoturismo,* Embratur, Brasilia, Brazil.

Gunn, C. 1994, *Tourism Planning: Basic Concept Cases, Third Edition,* Taylor & Francis, Washington D.C., USA.

Hawkins, D., Epler Wood, M. and Bittman, S. (eds.) 1995, *The Ecolodge Sourcebook for Planners and Developers,* The International Ecotourism Society, Burlington VT, USA.

Healy, R. 1992, *The Role of Tourism in Sustainable Development,* Center for Tropical Conservation, Duke University, NC, USA.

Higgins, B. 1996, 'The Global Structure of the Nature Tourism Industry: Ecotourists, Tour Operators, and Local Businesses', *Journal of Travel Research,* Vol. 25, No. 2, pp. 11-18.

Hillel, O. and de Oliveira, H. 2000, *Ecotourism Capacity Building Workshop,* Conservation International, Washington, USA.

Honey, M. 1999, *Ecotourism and Sustainable Development: Who owns paradise?,* Island Press, Washington D.C., USA.

Hoyt, E. 1994, *Whale Watching and the Community: The Way Forward,* Whale and Dolphin Conservation Society, Bath, UK.

Instituto Costarricense de Turismo 1997, *Certificación para la sostenibilidad turística CST: Guía de aplicación,* Instituto Costarricense de Turismo, Costa Rica.

Langholz, J. 1996. 'Economics, Objectives, and Success of Private Nature Reserves in Sub-Saharan Africa and Latin America.' Conservation Biology 10, no. 1: 271-80.

Lash, G., Austin, A. and Higgins, B., in press, Rural Ecotourism Assessment Program, The International Ecotourism Society, Burlington, VT, USA.

LEAD - Brazil *1999,* 'Sustainable tourism: a Brazilian perspective', a paper presented to the UN Commission on Sustainable Development, 7th Session, 19 – 30 April 1999, New York, USA.

Lewis, K. (in press), 'Operation and management' in: Mehta, H., Baez, A. and O'Loughlin, P. (eds.), *International Ecolodge Guidelines,* The International Ecotourism Society, Burlington, Vermont, USA.

Lindberg, K 1991, *Policies for Maximizing Nature Tourism's Ecological and Economic Benefits,* World Resources Institute, Washington D.C., USA

Lindberg, K. 1998, 'Economic aspects of ecotourism' in: Lindberg, K., Epler Wood, M. and Engeldrum, D. (eds.), *Ecotourism: A guide for planners and managers Volume 2,* The International Ecotourism Society, Burlington, VT, USA.

Lindberg, K. and Enriquez, J. 1994, *An analysis of ecotourism's economic contribution to conservation and development in Belize, Volume 1,* WWF (US), Washington D.C., USA.

Lindberg, K. and Huber, R. 1993, 'Economic issues in ecotourism management' in: Lindberg, K. and Hawkins, D. (eds.) 1993, *Ecotourism: A guide for planners and managers, Volume 1,* The International Ecotourism Society, Burlington, VT, USA.

Lindberg, K., Furze, B., Staff, M. and Black, R. 1998, *Ecotourism in the Asia Pacific Region: Issues and Outlook, FAO* Regional Office for Asia and the Pacific, Thailand.

McLaren, D. 1999, 'The history of indigenous peoples and tourism', *Cultural Survival Quarterly,* Vol. 23, No. 2, p. 27, Cultural Survival, Cambridge, MA, USA.

Mehta, H., Baez, A. and O'Loughlin (eds.) in press, *International Ecolodge Guidelines,* The International Ecotourism Society, Burlington, VT, USA.

Mesquita, C. and Aquirre, J. and Cifuentes, M.

and Müller, E. 2000, 'Caracterización de las reservas naturales provadas en América Latina' Revista Forestal Centroamericana, No. 30, April-June 2000.

Obermair, K. 1998, *Future Trends in Tourism: Alliance Internationales de Tourisme Delphi Study,* Alliance Internationales de Tourisme, Vienna.

RARE Center for Tropical Conservation 2000, *Nature Guide Training Program,* RARE Center for Tropical Conservation, Washington D.C., USA.

Scheyvens, R. 2000, 'Promoting Women's empowerment through involvement in ecotourism: Experiences in the third world', *Journal of Sustainable Tourism,* Vol. 8, No. 3, pp. 232 – 249.

SECA 2000, *European donor funding of ecotourism within environmental programmes,* SECA, Montpelier, France.

Shah, K. and Gupta, V. 2000, Working Paper: *Tourism, the Poor and Other Stakeholders: Experience in Asia,* Overseas Development Institute, UK.

Sirakaya, E., McLellen, R., Norman, W. and Toepper, L. 1996, *The results of the Ecotourism Operator Study,* The International Ecotourism Society, Burlington, VT, USA. Additionally online at www.ecotourism.org

Stankey, G., Cole, D., Lucas, R., Peterson, M. and Frissell, S. 1985, *The Limits of Acceptable Change (LAC) System for Wilderness Planning,* United States Department of Agriculture, USA.

Steck, B., Strasdas, W. and Gustedt, E. *1999, Tourism in Technical Cooperation: A guide to the conception, planning and implementation of project accompanying measures in regional rural development and nature conservation,* Deutsche Gesellschaft für Technische Zusammenarbeit (GTZ), Eschborn, Germany.

Strasdas, W. 2000, *Ecotourism in Nature Conservation Projects in Mexico and Belize,* Deutsche Gesellschaft füur Technische Zusammen arbeit (GTZ), Eschborn, Germany.

Stronza, A. 1999, 'Learning both ways: Lessons from a corporate and community ecotourism collaboration', *Cultural Survival Quarterly, Vol.* 23, No.2, pp. 36 – 39, Cultural Survival, Cambridge, MA, USA.

Stronza, A. 2000, *Because it is ours: Community-based ecotourism in the Peruvian Amazon,* a dissertation presented to University of Florida, Gainesville, FL, USA.

Sutton, M. 1999, 'Aboriginal ownership of national parks and tourism', *Cultural Survival Quarterly*, Vol. 23, No.2, pp. 55 – 56, Cultural Survival, Cambridge, MA, USA

Sweeting, J., Bruner, A. and Rosenfeld, A. 1999, *The Green Host Effect: An integrated approach to sustainable tourism and resort development*, Conservation International, Washington D.C., USA.

Tearfund 2000, *Tourism - an ethical issue: Market Research Report*, Tearfund, Middlesex, UK.

The International Ecotourism Society 1993 *Ecotourism Guidelines for Nature Tour Operators*, The International Ecotourism Society, Burlington, VT, USA.

Toledo, L. (ed.) Unpublished, *Brazil Technical Cooperation Program for the Development of Ecotourism in the Legal Amazon Region: PROECOTUR (BR-0208) Loan Proposal*, Inter-American Development Bank, Washington D.C., USA.

Travel Industry Association of America 2000, *Tourism works for America 2000*, Travel Industry Association of America, Washington D.C., USA.

Thresher, P., 1981, The present value of an Amboseli Lion, *World Animal Review*, 40:30-33.

U.S. Travel Data Center 1992, *Discover America: Tourism and the Environment*, Travel Industry Association of America, Washington D.C., USA.

Weaver, D. (ed.) 1998, *Ecotourism in the Less Developed World*, CAB International, Oxon, UK.

Weiler, B. and Ham, S. 1999, 'Training Ecotour Guides in Developing Countries: Lessons learned from Panama's first guides course' in: Hsu, C. (ed.), *New Frontiers in Tourism Research*, International Society of Travel and Tourism Educators Annual Conference, Proceedings of refereed papers Vol XI, Vancouver, Canada.

Wesche, R. and Drumm, A. 1999, *Defending the Rainforest*, Accion Amazonia, Quito, Ecuador.

Western, D. 1993, 'Defining Ecotourism', in: Lindberg, K. and Hawkins, D. (eds.), *Ecotourism: A guide for planners and managers Volume 1*, The International Ecotourism Society, Burlington, VT, USA.

Whelan, T. (ed.) 1991, *Nature Tourism: Managing for the Environment*, Island Press, Washington D.C., USA.

Wight, Pam A. 1996a, 'North American Ecotourists: Market Profile and Trip Characteristics', *Journal of Travel Research*. Spring, vol. 24 (4), pp. 2-10.

Wight, Pam A. 1996b, 'North American Ecotourism Markets: Motivations, Preferences and Destinations', *Journal of Travel Research*, vol. 25, pp. 3-10.

World Tourism Organization 1997, *Tourism 2020 Vision*, World Tourism Organization, Madrid, Spain.

World Tourism Organization 1997, *Tourism Highlights 1997*, World Tourism Organization, Madrid, Spain.

World Tourism Organization 1999, *Tourism Highlights 1999*, World Tourism Organization, Madrid, Spain.

World Tourism Organization 2000, *Tourism Highlights 2000*, World Tourism Organization, Madrid, Spain.

WWF 2000, *Tourism Certification: An analysis of Green Globe 21 and other tourism certification programs*, WWF, UK.

Ziffer, K. 1989, *Ecotourism: The Uneasy Alliance*, Conservation International, Washington D.C., USA.

Resource Organizations

Asociación Alianza Verde
Centro de información sobre la naturaleza, cultura y artesania de Peten
Castillo de Arismendi
Parque Central
Ciudad Flores, Peten, Guatemala
Tel: 502 926 0718
Fax: 502 926 0718
Email: saulblanco@yahoo.com
Contact: Saul Blanco, General Director

Asociación Ecuatoriana de Ecoturismo
Calle Victor Hugo E10-111 e Isla Pinzon
Ciudadela Jipijapa, Quito, Ecuador
Tel: 563 2 245055/466295
Fax: 563 2 245055/466295
Email: asec@accessinter.net
Contact: Raul Garcia, President

Alaska Wilderness Recreation and Tourism Association (AWRTA)
2207 Spenard Road, Suite 201
Anchorage, AK 99503, USA
Tel: 907 258 3171
Fax: 907 258 3851
Email: info@awrta.org
Website: www.awrta.org
Contact: Sarah Leonard, Executive Director

Baja Ecotourism and Sea Kayak Association
c/o Paddling South
PO Box 827
Calistonga, CA 94515, USA
Tel: 707 942 4550
Email: tourbaja@aol.com
Website: www.tourbaja.com
Contact: Trudi Angell, Secretary

Borneo Eco Tours
Shoplot 12A, 2nd Floor
Lorong Bernam 3,
Taman Soon Kiong
88300 Kota Kinabalu, Sabah, Malaysia
Tel: 60 88 234009
Fax: 60 88 233688
Email: albert@borneoecotours.com
Website: www.borneoecotours.com
Contact: Albert Teo, Managing Director

Brazilian Society for the Environment
Caixa Postal/PO Box 2432
Rio de Janerio CEP 20001-970, Brazil
Tel: 55 21 2210155
Fax: 55 21 2625946
Email: biosfera@mtec.com.br
Contact: Dorival Correla Bruni, President

Canodros S. A. / Kapawi Lodge
Luis Urdaneta 14-18 y Avenida Ejercito
Guayaquil, Ecuador
Tel: 593 4 280905
Fax: 593 4 287651
Email: eco-tourism1@canodros.com.ec
Website: www.canodros.com
Contact: Daniel Koupermann, Product Manager

Charles Darwin Foundation, Inc.
100 North Washington Street, Suite 232,
Falls Church, VA 22046, USA
Tel: 703 538 6833
Fax: 703 538 6835
Email: Darwin@galapagos.org
Website: www.galapagos.org
Contact: Johannah Barry, Executive Director
Erica Buck, Media and Outreach Director

Conservation International
Conservation Enterprise Dept
1919 M Street NW, Suite 600
Washington D.C. 20036, USA
Tel: 202 912 1421
Fax: 202 912 1030
Email: g.ryan@conservation.org

Website: www.conservation.org
Contact: Greta Ryan, Manager Global Ecotourism
Initiatives

Convention on Biological Diversity
393 St. Jacques Street, Suite 300
World Trade Center, Canada, H2Y 1N9
Tel: +1 514 288 2220
Fax: +1 514 288 6588
Email: secretariat@biodiv.org
Website: www.biodiv.org
Contact: Hamdallah Zedan, Executive Secretary

**Cooperative Research Centre for Sustainable
Tourism** / International Centre for Ecotourism
Research (ICER)
Griffith University
PMB 50, Gold Coast, Qld 9726, Australia
Tel: +61 7 55528675
Fax: +61 7 55528895
Email: r.buckley@mailbox.gu.edu.au
Website: www.gu.edu.au/centre/icer
Contact: Ralf Buckley, Director

Costa Rica Expeditions
Dept. 235/
PO Box 025216
Miami, FL 33102-5216, USA
Tel: 506 257 0766
Fax: 506 257 1665
Email: mskaye@expeditions.co.cr
Website: www.costaricaexpeditions.com
Contact: Michael Kaye, CEO

**Deutsche Gesellscharft für Technische
Zusammenarbeit (GTZ)**
Division 44 (Environmental Management, Water,
Energy, Transport)
Postfach 5180
65726 Eschborn, Germany
Tel: +49 6196 791356
Fax: +49 6196 797151
Email: burghard.rauschelbach@gtz.de
Contact: Burghard Rauschelbach, Senior Advisor

Ecobrasil
Caixa Postal 14551
22412-970 Rio de Janeiro RJ
Tel: 55 (21) 2422 6228 or 2512 4187
Email: ariane@ecobrasil.org.br
econews@ecobrasil.org.br
Contact: Ariane Janér

Ecological Tourism in Europe (EETE)
Am Michaelshof 8-10
D-53177 Bonn, Germany
Tel: +49 (0) 228 359008
Fax: +49 (0) 228 359096
Email: OeTE-Bonn@t-online.de
Contact: Michael Meyer, Member of the Board

Ecotourism Association of Australia
GPO Box 268
Brisbane QLD 4001, Australia
Tel: 61 7 32295550
Fax: 61 7 32295255
Email: mail@ecotourism.org.au
Website: www.ecotourism.org.au
Contact: Keith Williams, Executive Officer

Ecotourism Society of Kenya
PO Box 10146,
00100 – Nairobi, Kenya
Tel: 254-2-331286
Fax: 254-2-218402
Email: info@esok.org
Website: www.esok.org
Contact: Judy Kepher-Gona, National Liaison
Officer

Ecotourism Society of Pakistan
5 Haroon Road Saroba Gardents
17 KM Ferozpur Road
Lahore, Pakistan
Tel: 92 42 5810850
Email: eco.tourism@comsats.net.pk
Website: www.ecotourism.org.pk
Contact: Ekrar Haroon, President

Ecotourism Society of Saskatchewan
3831 Gordon Rd
Regina SK S4S 5X3, Canada
Tel: 306 751 0120
Fax: 306 585 0614
Email: Hnaj@sk.sympatico.ca
Website: www.ecotourism.sk.ca
Contact: Joseph Hnatiuk, President

**ECOTRANS (The European Network
for Sustainable Tourism Development)**
Berliner Promenade 7
D-66111 Saarbrücken, Germany
Tel: +49 (0) 681 374679
Fax: +49 (0) 681 374633
Email: info@ecotrans.de
Website: www.ecotrans.org
Contact: Herbert Hamele, President

Edward D. Stone Jr. & Associates (E.S.D.A.)
1512 E. Broward Blvd. Suite 110
Ft. Lauderdale, FL 33301, USA
Tel: 954 524 3330
Fax: 954 524 0177
Email: hmehta@edsaplan.com
Contact: Hitesh Mehta, Ecotourism Studio

ETC Asia Co., Ltd (An Asia Web Direct Company)
Muang Mai Chrysler Building, 4th Floor
9/17 Moo 6 Thepkasattri Road
T. Rasada A. Muang
Phuket 83000, Thailand
Tel: + 66 76 236550

Fax: + 66 76 236542
Email: noah@etc-etcetera.com
Website: www.etc-etcetera.com
Contact: Noah Shepherd, Managing Director

**Fundacion Pachamama / The Pachamama
Alliance**
PO Box 29291, Presidio Bldg. #1007, Suite 215
San Francisco, CA 94129-9191, USA
Tel: 415 561 4522
Fax: 415 561 4521
Email: info@pachamama.org
Website: www.pachamama.org

Honduras Ecotourism Association
Programa de Becas
CAPS/HOPS/USAID
3 er Piso Edif Gomez Zuniga
Colonia Alamaeda
Tegucigalpa, Honduras
Tel: 504 31 4303 / 4258
Fax: 504 31 4419
Website: www.txinfinet.com/mader/ecotravel/
center/honduras/aproecoh.html
Contact: Luis Tinoco

Horizontes Nature Tours
PO Box 1780 – 1002 P.E.
San José, Costa Rica
Tel: 506 222 2022
Fax: 506 255 4513
Email: horizont@racsa.co.cr
Website: www.horizontes.com
Contact: Tamara Budowski, President

Inter-American Investment Corp
1300 New York Ave NW
Washington DC 20577, USA
Tel: 202 623 3948
Fax: 202 623 3815
E-mail: iicmail@iadb.org
Website: www.iadb.org
Contact: Jorge Roldan, Chief Economist

International Expeditions
13540 Route 108,
Highland MD 20777, USA
Tel: 301 854 3096
Fax: 301 854 3096
Email: sholleyc@aol.com
Website: www.ietravel.com
Contact: Craig Sholley, Director of Conservation
and Education

**International Galapagos Tour Operator
Association (IGTOA)**
c/o Voyagers International
P.O. Box 915, Ithaca,
NY 14851, USA
Tel: 607-273-4321
Fax: 607-273-3873

E-mail: dave@voyagers.com
Website: www.voyagers.com
Contact: Dave Blanton, President

Japan Ecotourism Society (JES)
4-6-4 Shibaura, Minato-ku
Tokyo 108-0023, Japan
Tel: 81 3 54396046
Fax: 81 3 54396053
Email: ecojapan@alles.or.jp
Website: www.ecotourism.gr.jp/indexenglish.htm
Contact: Hiroko Kobayashi, Vice Secretary-General

Kenya Association of Tour Operators (KATO)
3rd Floor, Hughes Building,
Nairobi, Kenya
Email: kato@africaonline.co.ke
Website: www.katokenya.org
Contact: Fred Kaigwa

Lindblad Expeditions
1415 Western Avenue, Suite 700
Seattle, WA 98101, USA
Tel: 206 624 7750
Fax: 206 382 9594
Email: tomo@expeditions.com
Website: www.expeditions.com
Contact: Tom O'Brien, Director of Environmental
Affairs

Namibia Community Based Tourism
PO Box 86099
18 Liliencron Street, Windhoek, Namibia
Tel: 264 (0) 61 250558
Fax: 264 (0) 61222647
Email: nacobta@iafrica.com.na

Overseas Development Institute
Rural Policy and Environment Group
111 Westminster Bridge Road
London SE1 7JD, England
Tel: 44 (0) 20 7922 0300
Fax: 44 (0) 20 7922 0399
Email: c.Ashley@odi.org.uk
Website: www.odi.org.uk/rpeg/tourism.html
Contact: Caroline Ashley, Research Fellow

Planeta.com
Email: ron@planeta.com
Website: www.planeta.com
Contact: Ron Mader, Director

Rainforest Expeditions
Project Development
Aramburu 166, 4B
Lima 18, Peru
Tel: +51 1 421 8347
Fax: +51 1 421 8183
Email: nycander@rainforest.com.pe
Website: www.perunature.com
Contact: Eduardo Nycander, Manager

RARE Center for Tropical Conservation
1840 Wilson Blvd., Suite 402
Arlington VA 22201-3000, USA
Tel: 703 522 5070
Fax: 703 522 5027
Email: rare@rarecenter.org
Website: www.rarecenter.org
Contact: Brett Jenks, President

Rethinking Tourism
366 North Prior Avenue, Suite 203
Saint Paul, MN 55104, USA
Tel: 651 644 9984
Fax: 651 644 9984
Email: rtproject@aol.com
Website: www2.planeta.com/mader/ecotravel/
resources/rtp/rtp.html
Contact: Deborah McLaren, Director

Studienkreis für Tourismus und Entwicklung e.V
Institute for Tourism and Development
Kapellenweg 3
D – 82541 Ammerland, Germany
Tel: +49 (0) 8177 1783
Fax: +49 (0) 8177 1349
Email: studienkreistourismus@compuserve.com
Website: www.studienkreis.org
Contact: Dr. Dietlind vVon Lab?berg, General
Manager

The Ecotourism Society Philippines
Foundation
1357 JP Laurel St
San Miguel Manila, Philippines
Tel: 632 736 3838/40
Fax: 632 736 3839
Email: wsp710@i-next.net
Contact: Mina Gabor, President

The Fiji Ecotourism Association
PO Box U9
Laucala Bay campus
Suva Fiji
Fvb house
Thomson st. (cnr Scott st.) Suva Fiji
Tel: 679 307677
Fax: 679 307140
Email: ecotourism@is.com.fj
Contact: Rashida Sahib

The International Ecotourism Society
PO Box 668,
Burlington, VT 05402, USA
Tel: 802 651 9818
Fax: 802 651 9819
Email: ecomail@ecotourism.org
Website: www.ecotourism.org

The Nature Conservancy
International Conservation Program
4245 North Fairfax Drive

Arlington VA 22203-1606, USA
Tel: 703 841 8177
Fax: 703 841 4880
Email: adrumm@tnc.org
Website: www.tnc.org/ecotourism
Contact: Andy Drumm, Ecotourism Director

The Swedish Ecotourism Society
Box 39
Morsil 83004, Sweden
Tel: 46 647 660025
Fax: 46 647 660025
Email: info@ekoturismforeningen.a.se
Website: www.ekoturism.org
Contact: Maria Kjellstrom

Tourism Concern
Stapleton House
277-281 Holloway Road
London N7 8Hn, England
Tel: 0207 753 3330
Fax: 0207 753 3331
Email: info@tourismconcern.org.uk
Website: www.tourismconcern.org.uk
Contact: Patricia Barnett, Director

Tourism Watch
Church Development Service (EED)
PO Box 10 03 40
70747 Leinfelden-Echterdingen, Germany
Tel: +49 (0) 711 7989 281
Fax: +49 (0) 711 7989 283
Email: tourism-watch@due.org
www.tourism-watch.org
Contact: Heinz Fuchs, Director

Tropic Ecological Adventures /
Accion Amazonia
PO Box 17 21 508
Quito, Ecuador
Tel: +593 (2) 225 907
Fax: +593 (2) 560 756
Email: acciona@ecnet.ec
Contact: Sofia Darquea, Managing Director

United Nations Environment Programme
Division of Technology, Industry & Economics
Production and Consumption Unit
Tour Mirabeau, 39-43 Quai Andre Citroen
75739 Paris, France
Tel: (33 1) 44 37 14 50
Fax: (33 1) 44 37 14 74
Email: unep.tie@unep.fr
Website: www.unepie.org/tourism/home.html
Contact: Oliver Hillel, Tourism Programme
Coordinator

Virginia EcoTourism Association
PO Box 8754
Virginia Beach VA 23450-8754, USA
Tel:757.427.4209

Fax: 757.471.2330
Email mail@veta.net
Website: www.veta.net
Contact: Pete Hangen

Wilderness Travel
1102 Ninth Street
Berkeley, CA 94710, USA
Tel: 510 558 2488
Fax: 510 558 2489
Email: info@wildernesstravel.com
Website: www.wildernesstravel.com
Contact: Barbara Banks, Director of Marketing
and New Trip Development

Wolfgang Strasdas
Independent Consultant
Environmental Planner
Palmstr. 13
80469 Muünchen 80469, Germany
Tel: +49 89 2015115
Fax: +49 89 8631266
Email: sStrasdasW@aol.com
Contact: Dr Wolfgang Strasdas

World Tourism Organization
Capitan Haya 42
28020 Madrid, Spain
Tel; 34 91 567 8100
Fax: 34 91 571 3733
Email: omt@world-tourism.org
www.world-tourism.org
Contact: Eungenio Yunis, Chief of Sustainable
Development of Tourism Section

WWF-Brazil
Conservation Department
SHIS EQ QL 6/8
Conj. E – 20 andar – Brasilia/ DF 71620 – 430, Brazil
Tel: +55 61 364 7400
Fax: +55 61 364 7474
Email: sergio@wwf.org.br
Website: www.wwf.org.br
Contact: Sérgio Salazar Salvati, Program Officer
Ecotourism

WWF International
Conservation Policy
Avenue du Mont Blanc,

1196 Gland, Switzerland
Tel: +41 22 364 9207
Fax: +41 22 364 5829
Email: jheap@wwfint.org
Contact: Jenny Heap, Director

WWF Mediterranean Program
Via Po 25C, 00186 Rome, Italy
Tel: +39 0 684497339
Fax: +39 0 68413866
Email: pdebrine@wwfmedpo.org
Contact: Peter DeBrine, Tourism Initiative
Coordinator

WWF-United Kingdom
Business and Consumption Unit
Panda House
Weyside Park
Catteshall Lane, Godalming
Surrey GU7 1XR, England
Tel: +44 (0) 1483 412 508
Fax: +44 (0) 1483 861 360
Email: jwoolford@wwf.org.uk
Contact: Justin Woolford, Tourism Policy Officer